THE SECRET LETTERS OF PRESIDENT DONALD J. TRUMP, AGE 72 1/6

Praises for The Secret Letters of President Donald Trump, Age 72 1/6.

"Rudolf Hess should be arrested and locked up for breaking into president Donald Trump's brain. How he came out alive is something that I'm sure the Russians are investigating."
—*New York Daily Apple*

"Don't pick this book up unless you are willing to let reason, your reason, crumble as soon as laughter tickles it."
—*Miami Bell*

"Rudolf t.g. Hess must have been dropped on a hard floor when he was a toddler. There is no other way to explain his unique madness."
—*Washington Ghostwriters*

"You must not read this fucking book if you do not want to be offended. LOL. I'm not kidding." —*London Daily Chips*

"If you do not find yourself screaming at some of these letters, then you are a conscientious objector carried away by your chuckles."
—*Publishers' Slush Pile*

"For making me spill my coffee on my pants, sorry, groin, I say fuck eight generations of your ancestors."
—*Moscow Golden Shower Times*

"Be ready for your conscience to lose its virginity before you open this book. You will not come out the same way you went in, even if you were President Donald Trump."
—*European Rags of Paris*

"Rudolf t.g. Hess has sprinkled lies into non-fiction the same way Bill Cosby sprinkled drugs into women's drinks, with the same effect."
—*Philadelphia Evening Answers*

"This Trump is smarter than the one in the White House."
Grace Upbeat, the author of *My Nuclear Button Is Bigger than Yours*.

"For spending this much time inside Trump's head, I hope Rudolf t.g. Hess is forced to pay rent." – Tony Bacharach, DC Attorney.

"I don't care who you are, this Trump will surprise you in some pleasant ways as you read these letters. Sometimes, against his best interest, he is really really pee your pant funny." - Jasper Bush, Rock Musician.

"Finally, I understood Donald Trump's mind. Thank you, Mr. Hess." – Michael York, Homeless New Yorker.

THE SECRET LETTERS OF PRESIDENT DONALD J. TRUMP, AGE 72 1/6

**Yours truly,
Donald J. Trump**
(45th President of the United States of America)

Rudolf t.g. Hess

Jointly published by
Noirledge Limited, under its Winepress Publishing imprint
and Irokopost Media Group Inc., Rosedale, NY 11422

Noirledge Limited
13, Elewura Street, off Lagos Bypass, Challenge, Ibadan
Tel: +234 809 816 4359 | +234 805 316 4359
Email: press@winepress.pub | www.winepress.pub

Copyright © Rudolf Ogoo Okonkwo, 2019
Rudolf Ogoo Okonkwo asserts the moral right to be identified as the author of this work.

ISBN: 978-0-9768354-8-6
A catalogue record for this book is available from the National Library of Nigeria.

All rights reserved. No part of this publication may be reproduced, stored in or introduced into a retrieval system, or transmitted, in any form or by any means, electronic, mechanical, photocopying, recording or otherwise, without prior permission in writing from Irokopost Media Group Inc. and the copyright owner. Any unauthorised distribution or use of this publication may be a direct infringement of the author's and publisher's rights, and those responsible may be liable in law accordingly.

Cover Concept: Gabriel Agema
Cover Design: Servio Gbadamosi
Book Design: Servio Gbadamosi
Typesetting: www.noirledge.com

Dedication

To
Edna, my wife
For the decorations you brought to my life.
There is no better book to dedicate to you than this one.

There is a fat worm in these waters
In these lands a predatory worm:
He ate the Island's flag
Hoisting up his overseer's banner,
He was nourished from the captive blood
Of the poor buried patriots.

—Muños Marín by Pablo Neruda

Contents

You've read his tweets, but have you read his letters? If his tweets were that bombastic, how would his secret letters be? Welcome in.

Dedication	7
Renunciation	13
How I Got Possession of Donald Trump's Secret Letters	15

Donald Trump's Letters to:

1. Barron Trump's teacher — 21
2. Hillary Clinton — 26
3. Chris Matthews — 29
4. Pope Francis — 33
5. God — 37
6. Stormy Daniels — 42
7. Dr. Martin Luther King Jr. — 44
8. Vladimir Putin — 49
9. Allah — 54
10. Michael Cohen — 58
11. Nelson Mandela — 62
12. Barack Obama — 66
13. Mark Cuban — 70
14. Gen. Michael Flynn — 73
15. Rosie O'Donnell — 77
16. Fred Trump — 81
17. Kanye West — 86

18. Melania Trump	91
19. Jeff Sessions	94
20. Ivanka Trump	97
21. Mysterious woman	99
22. Rex Tillerson	102
23. John McCain	104
24. Emmanuel Macron	107
25. Oprah Winfrey	113
26. Prince Harry	118
27. Kim Jong-un	120
28. Kid separated from parents at the US border	122
29. Roseanne Barr	125
30. Queen Elizabeth	128
31. President of Croatia	132
32. Putin 2nd Letter	135
33. LeBron James	137
34. Omarosa	139
35. Paul Manafort	142
36. Michael Cohen 2nd Letter	145
37. Mike Pompoe	146
38. Barron Trump	148
Acknowledgment	151

Renunciation

Because in today's world we have to warn customers to eat the bread and not the plastic wrap and to drink very hot coffee slowly and not in one go, it is necessary to state here that this book is a work of satire.

You know, the way a short story is fiction. Yeah! But these days, you need to make it clear, else someone calls it fake news.

So, let me make it abundantly clear. Some names in this book are real names. What is not real is the name of the author. Some events depicted in this book actually happened. What did not actually happen is what the author of the letters thinks about these events. Okay, we don't know if it happened. It could have. Considering…

Believe me, we do not need authorization to break into the brain of anyone and take up residence. After all, every night when we dream, people, imaginary and real, break into our subconscious minds to interact with us.

That is all that I have done here.

Any character that feels a little defamed should take a second look at the fame this work bestowed upon him or her. Anyone who feels a little bit libeled should consider that by making an appearance here, his or her place in high-end literature is secured.

I'm sorry that I have to say all these at the end of the book. (My God, I hope they did not trick me and put this at the beginning of the book despite my protest.) I just don't want to deface the book's opening pages by putting what is so obvious at the front.

I hope you will not demand a refund of your money—Amazon takes 55 percent, just so you know. And I'm sure it is part of their First Amendment rights.

Now, please close the book gently. I didn't say you should flip it on the desk. Close gently.

Thank you.

Now think deeply about what you have read—no, not this renunciation. I mean, the whole book. I bet you, it will soon begin to make sense. Yeah, it is that kind of a book.

As you do so, stay tuned for more works from the Wiseguy Satire Series. And thank you for taking this ride with me.

How I Got Possession of Donald Trump's Secret Letters

On the day Rachel Maddow of MSNBC got ahold of the exclusive story that two pages of president Donald Trump's 2005 tax papers were in the hands of a journalist, David Cay Johnston, I was one of the four million people who were glued to the TV watching and waiting for her to reveal the contents of the tax papers.

I made popcorn and lemonade, took off my shoes, and sat on the couch with my legs propped up. I set my cell phone on vibrate to escape the ringing of friends who would want to discuss the matter before the presentation was finished.

As Rachel dragged it on and on, milking it for ratings purposes, I flipped through other channels and back to her. At one point, I decided to write a comment on her show's MSNBC website.

"Get on with it, Rachel. Stop having an orgasm on live TV over Donald Trump's 2005 tax papers. You liberals are easily fooled. What if the tax papers were not sent to the journalist by a whistleblower? What if they were sent to him by Donald Trump himself?"

I posted the comment and waited. After about five minutes, I deleted the comment. I was getting paranoid over American liberals. I did not want anyone to come after me.

But it was too late.

I watched Mr. Johnston reveal that Trump paid a 25 percent effective tax rate. The total amount was $38 million. The 25 percent rate, which is respectable for American billionaires, always eager to avoid paying taxes, strengthened my suspicion that Trump could have released the tax papers himself to distract the country from the ongoing Russian investigation.

I was glad I deleted my post.

As a relatively unknown journalist, I was slightly jealous of Mr. Johnston. His possession of Trump's 2005 tax returns had once again brought him national limelight, especially for those who were not of age when he won the 2001 Pulitzer Prize for Beat Reporting. I was sure even if he did not want it to, the exposure would increase the sale for his best-selling book on taxes. It was the kind of break I needed. In these challenging days of journalism, any opportunity that a reporter gets must be maximized before the gig economy swallows us all.

I thought about Johnston's story and how he got the tax papers. According to him, he got a call from home that some documents came in the mail that he needed to see. He left his assignment post and returned home. When he opened the package, it was Donald Trump's tax papers.

He did not satisfactorily answer the question, "Why him?" He had known Trump for decades and was an investigative reporter who had written several books on taxes and how the American tax system favors the rich at the expense of the poor. But he was not the only one who had such a reputation.

One year after, I had forgotten about Rachael Maddow's not-so-big-revelation. Like many Americans, I had endured another unrealized expectation, as the tax revelation did nothing to move the needle of public opinion anywhere close to making president Donald Trump see the need for himself to release his tax returns.

And that was when the email came.

I could not identify the email address Wiseguysatire@gmail.com. I almost deleted it because of the title: "Today is your lucky day."

My hunch was that it must be one of those Nigerian scams or Eastern European phishing emails. I was sure it would talk about a fortune of a prince or president in Africa that I would get a share of if I helped move some money abroad. Or it could be a random lottery I had won without ever submitting my name. Knowing the endless creativity of these scammers, it could be someone selling Viagra over the Internet.

Just because I had never seen this particular title, I opened the email:

> Hey Rudi,
> Today is your lucky day. We saw what you wrote on the MSNBC website and we think that you are the right man to receive "The Secret Letters of Donald Trump" and share them with the world. Are you interested? If you are, just click reply.

The first question that came to my mind was, what did I write on the MSNBC website? I could not recall at that point. Like I said, it had been over a year ago.

But because I had no penchant for writing comments on websites, I flashed back and could recall what I wrote. But I had deleted it almost immediately.

Some years back, I had played along with one of the scammers who wanted help to move money from Senegal after his father died. I not only enjoyed my conversation with him, but I also was able to extract an article out of it. Remembering that, I decided to play along with this group.

I replied with a request to be reminded of what I wrote on MSNBC.

I soon got an email back that simply pasted the exact comment that I wrote—word for word.

Sweat seeped through the pores of my skin as I read. It did not make sense. Even if I did not delete the comment, just considering the number of comments made on the website on that day, why me? And how did they get my email address? I did not register on the website with my real name or my real email address. But the email they sent came to my real email address.

What else did they know about me? I had numerous questions. Just while I was still composing an email full of questions for them, I got another email. This one was brief.

"Are you in or out?"

At this point, my journalistic instinct kicked in. I wrote back that I was in.

"Great! We know your questions. We have no time to answer them. We will send you the letters as we capture them. If you like them, get them published and your career will be great again. If you don't like them, delete them and you will never hear from us. But if you choose to publish them, do not alter them. Publish as they are."

I desperately wanted to ask just one question, but they shut me down. It wasn't about how they got the letters or who owns the copyrights. It wasn't about how I would be able to prove to the world that they were authentic.

I consoled myself by just remembering that these were the same questions David Cay Johnston confronted when he got Donald Trump's 2015 tax returns in the mail.

As I prepared the letters for publication, more of them came in. It appears as if the people sending these letters were getting them as President Trump was writing them. Maybe they have control of his computer screen or the screen of whatever tool he was using to write the letters.

I guess with their publication, Trump will know his letters have been leaking out. So here are the secret letters of president Donald Trump.

Letters

Donald Trump's Letter to His Son's Teacher

Tuesday, March 20, 2018

Dear Teacher,

Today is the birthday of my son, Barron. I write you today because I need your help to teach my amazing son, Barron, some universal truths that I subscribe to and highly recommend for any young man who wants to be a success in America. I'm living proof that you don't need to fight in Vietnam or Iraq or Afghanistan to be a success. Believe me, those days are gone.

My son is a fantastic kid, just like his father. I would have taught him myself, but I am very busy running the country, making our America great again. It is a super tremendous responsibility, and I am sure that you appreciate my wholesome dedication to the task. I'm bigly kicking butts and giving the enemies of America hell. Dear teacher, don't teach him that Cold War era nonsense that I was taught at the Wharton School about Russia being an enemy of America.

No one really knows, but I suspect that my son is watching the filth that the fake news media are peddling about me. Stormy Daniels. Karen McDougal. Nasty people. Terrible! I'm talking about all the salacious and bigoted lies they tell about a magnificent person like me. Very sad! How could more people have watched that disgrace of an interview that Stormy Daniels had with CNN's Anderson Cooper, than my classy *60 Minutes* interview? The pit of hell that is the Internet is full of those types. Dear teacher, we need to do something about it. Please, steer my son toward the very few sophisticated and right channels left in American media, like Fox News and Breitbart news site. Do it, and half of the job will be done.

He is a good guy, my son. I'm sure he will listen to you more than he listens to Melania or myself. He resists, even though deep inside him, I know that I'm the greatest superhero he knows. I see it in the way he looks at me in awe when it is raining and I hold up the umbrella and he follows behind. If you doubt me, ask him to name his greatest hero and watch him gush about me and the great feats that I am accomplishing for America each blessed day to the astonishment of our enemies both foreign and domestic. Wonderful job I'm doing. Even the fake news CNN agrees that it is hugely unprecedented.

I write this letter not because Abraham Lincoln wrote one. I'm sure you know about it. By the way, mine is more terrific. Senator Orrin Hatch already said that I am smarter than Abraham Lincoln and George Washington put together. If you like, throw in Barack Obama. So, there is no contest here. I write this letter because of something very, very important to me. I don't want all these women coming on TV and talking trash about me to affect my boy and his relationship with women. Quite unfair! As I look at him, I'm worried that he is picking up the softness of his mother. That will be a total disaster. I want him to, instead, pick up the sternness of my beloved, Ivanka—my perpetual Miss Universe. She is a tough cookie, like her father. She is a maestro in the art of the deal.

I want my boy to be crazy enough to believe in himself and the possibilities of everything his mind conjures. That is 100 percent true. Did I mention that he is destined to be a winner? I would hate to see him toe the lines of those lightweight "monkey see, monkey do" types that are common with lazy African-American people. I want him to be as smooth as a real estate salesman, a successful one at that, not the heavily indebted Jared Kushner types. Let the failures amongst his peers waste the low energy they have (just like Mitt Romney and Jeb Bush) talking about him while he soars to great heights that his father has carved out for him from nothing. Believe me, the $1 million loan from my father in 1975 is nothing compared to the billions and billions that I have today. Teach him that humility is totally overrated. Once he knows that, it is all he needs to be unstoppable. Not even ten Robert Muellers can stop him.

I want him to grow up looking at my face on Mount Rushmore and all the luxurious monuments created in my name and admire them with pride. Teach him to measure success by how freaking tall and large his houses are, and how marvelously beautiful his women are. When all is said and done, those are the only things that matter. Frankly, the rest of human postulations, like the spirit behind the Paris Agreement, are mere superstitions. Trust me, a kiss is a more tangible commodity than a soul. Build a great wall inside him to separate him from those out-of-control simpletons who think otherwise. I bet you, he will figure out how to make those simpletons pay for the wall.

Teach him not to aim for the stars, but to be the star, the brightest that God ever created. He may be twelve now, but soon, he will know the difference. Those dumb morons who aim for the stars get burnt, but those who become a star, like reality stars—how do I say this mildly—have women throwing panties at them on stage. That is where I want my son to be—in the same orbit with Princess Diana. When it comes to women, remind him of that great quote of mine: "If you need Viagra, you're probably with the wrong girls." Believe me, an orgasm is the closest anyone has been to heaven.

Teach him the rules of the good life. They are incredibly important. The weak serve the strong, the cowards take orders from the brave, and the victims soak the field of the heroes with their tears. Let my boy know that for him to be in the big league, it pays to be the menace. The best scenario is always the one that makes him come out on top. By the way, let him know that the only battle lost is the one fought with empathy. Let those with sickle cell help those with seizure disorders. We the good breeds are preordained to have a perfect life. It may be shocking to people, but he should not apologize for being perfect. It is not our fault.

    My whole life is about drama subdued. Teach him to be at home with drama. Let drama energize him and trigger his antennas to stay alert. There is no higher order. It is in that sphere, like on a golf course, that he will find a lot of people. Teach him to sieve the fake and bad people in the heat of the drama. Let him not cry for those who must be fired. He must learn that regret and apology are disgraceful habits. Tell him that there is always another option even after the final answer.

    When it comes to his obligation to America, teach him to hold close to his heart America first. Teach him not to be lured by the antics of people from some exotic lands. Let me tell you, those crooked and dangerous types have zero American homegrown skills. Their values are incompatible with our great American values. Teach him that it is not true that any way people worship God is valid. Okay? If that were true, I wouldn't have divorced Ivana and Maria, my first two wives. Some gods demand specific and rigorous catechism. And some other gods like their women as meek as Melania.

    Let my son understand why I said that those exotic people in our country should go back home. To be honest with you, teach him that I'm trying to help them pay a debt they owe to the roads. In the words of *This American Life Sef*'s writer, "Every sojourner owes a debt/To the roads, the rivers/And the spirits that pilot the stars. /But the debt that lives in whispers/Is the debt of return…" You see, it is one of their own that said it, not me. My noble goal is to help them pay the debt of return.

    Above all, teach my son to love himself. There is nobody bigger and better in loving himself than me, his father. Everybody likes me because of that. If he fails to love himself because of what people may say, he will end up a loser. And I don't want my son to be a loser, like Crooked Hillary Clinton, Weak Mitt Romney, and Lying James Comey. It will be totally embarrassing if it should happen to my son. The Trumps are the best in the world.

People are telling me that my son has got my great brain, so he is as smart as his father. Your job is to pull out of him the things that make him come alive. The rest will be easy. For I know, and you know, that he is not like all those stupid lads that you teach. He will answer his father's name—Trump the Great.

Dear teacher, do this for me, and I will give you the greatest deal of your life—a blanket pardon for past, present, and future infractions. Believe me, Paul Manafort would die for this.

Yours truly,
Donald J. Trump
The 45th President of the United States of America

Donald Trump's Letter to Hillary Clinton

Saturday, March 24, 2018

Hi Hillary,

I know that you will be surprised to receive this letter from me. I am that generous, you know. Despite what the liberal media wants the world to think of me, I am a practical Queens, New York, kid who made good on his promise to his father. That is what it is all about for us from our part of town. Nothing personal. In our pursuit of success, we treat anyone in our way as an enemy combatant.

I've attained the pinnacle of self-actualization. You may not understand the feeling because it is somewhere you will never get to. I can imagine the bitterness you must feel having aimed for the glass ceiling with a sledgehammer. Your swing at it and your failure to shatter it must have left you scarred for life. Sad!

I recognize that. And I have resolved to do something to reduce the pain. Won't that be marvelous?

We used to be cool, Hillary. Remember that I used to donate to your political campaigns. You and Bill came to some of my weddings—I don't remember which ones. What really happened? Where did things fall apart?

I guess it is politics. In my quiet moments, I wonder how we ended up where we are now. Deep inside me, that I call you

"Crooked Hillary" does not make me feel good. I want to make that clear. Even though your history is full of crooked things you and Bill did, who doesn't have such a dark history?

Bill has Monica Lewinsky. I have Stormy Daniels. Bill has Gennifer Flowers. I have Karen McDougal. Frankly, there is nothing new about any of this stuff.

Here is my plan: after I win the re-election, I want to change things. I want to return to that jolly good fellow that you used to run after for campaign money. Melania said that I have become a monster. And that made me feel sad. Though, personally, I do not think that I have changed. I think that now she has the opportunity to follow my activities, including words that I say. Before she was just interested in fashion, shoes, leggings, makeup, and hats.

But, then, even Ivanka is beginning to despise some of my recent decisions. And that is unacceptable to me. You know how I feel about Ivanka. Isn't she classy?

As part of my plan, I will invite you and Bill to the White House. I can even throw in Barack and Michelle Obama. Who knows? It depends on how I feel that day. I mean, we can have a happy White House reunion. If Jimmy Carter is still alive then, even though I doubt it, I will invite him too. And maybe George W. Bush too. Why not? There must be a place for failed presidents.

To be honest with you, it sometimes feels lonely here. Nobody around here understands the extent of the burden that I bear. All that I have around me are people who think I am a moron and an idiot. Meanwhile, the people who have been here, like you and Bill, people who really understand what I am going through, are not talking to me. It sucks.

By the time we have the meeting, I must have done all the things that my native constituents demand of me. You know them very well. The people you and Obama aptly described as bitter, Bible-clinging, gun-carrying baskets of deplorables. Once I build the wall for them and imprison them in their miserable world of yesterday, like Native Americans, we will go ahead and move the nation forward.

That will be a great time to unify the country. I will be up for healings of any kind. If need be, I will smoke a cigar with your husband, Bill. I will give you a shoulder massage if that will help. It is going to be better than the weak massage Joe Biden gives. I'm talking about healing, full healing for us all. I will be born again.

At that point, I will stop talking about Mueller investigating your ties with Russia. I will also stop demanding that you should be locked up for your email scandal. But until then, you will remain my reliable bogeyman. I will keep calling you "Crooked Hillary."

But lest be assured that it will come to an end one day.

Until then, I'm your president.

Yours truly,
Donald J. Trump
The 45th President of the United States

Donald Trump's Letter to Chris Matthews

Saturday, March 24, 2018

Hi Chris,

How is reality looking from the very bottom of the mainstream fake news media where you are gasping for air? Truth be told, I have been a lifeline for all you low-ratings shows. In another one year of watching every step that I take, I am sure you will experience a different kind of thrill going up your lightweight leg.

I will give it to you – at least you are not sleepy like that Todd Chuck, or is it Chuck Todd? I do flip through your show some days to see if spits have started hanging down your lips.

I write just to let you in on a big scoop. Oh yeah. This one will blow your mind. Piers Morgan has just nominated me for the 2018 Nobel Prize for Peace. It is happening, baby. Just in case you have not figured it out – it is for my work in unifying the Korean peninsula, and also for solving a problem that no American president in the last sixty years could solve, which is to end the Korean War and denuclearize the Korean peninsula.

Please tell me what is left for me to do to impress you mainstream media types. In less than one and half years in power, I solved what Obama called the most difficult problem I would face as president. The rest, like Mueller and Melania, are minor league.

I have ordered the National Parks Department to begin work on putting the face of Donald J. Trump on Mount Rushmore. I hope you will support the move when it is leaked to the media. Even if you don't, it is going up anyway. I have given the order. Your support is irrelevant. By the time you all get to hear about it and begin your usual kick at the blue sky, I will be in Oslo, Norway, accepting the Nobel Peace Prize. Who knows, I may decide to come back from Norway with some good journalists to replace some of you fake news people. I'm unstoppable.

So, your darling Bill Cosby has been convicted. The original nigga will spend the rest of his life in prison. I wonder why we cannot send one of you journalists to prison, just like Bill Cosby, as an example of what could happen to fake news peddlers? I want to start with one of your people at MSNBC. I don't remember his name, but he tweeted, "Cosby convicted, heading to prison. Finally, there is hope for Donald Trump." For a tweet like this, that man should be locked up for life. How dare he compare me with Cosby?

Cosby is such a weak, and I must say, foolish man. How could you have the level of success and fame that he had and still resort to sprinkling drugs in women's drinks? I don't get it. Like I told Billy Bush, I am a man's man. I know my worth. I know that women want me. And I know how to go after them aggressively when I need to. I don't need the aid of any substance to make my move. That was so dumb of Cosby. He is a Philadelphia guy like you. I hope you are not into that kind of lifestyle.

So, I have seen you talk about Stormy Daniels as if you don't have your own Stormy Daniels. Why are all you liberals like this? Your CNBC people even paid hush money of about $40,000 to your accuser. And that is for making inappropriate jokes and comments. Imagine if I have to pay for such jokes and comments. It would be in billions of dollars. So, I actually got a great deal for my $130,000 payout to that woman. The bottom line is that I did not have any abnormal relationship with that woman.

Look at how Matt Lauer crumbled. Shameful! I knew that guy was plastic. I could see beyond his facade. He looked like the type that would sprinkle drugs into women's drinks. But when the lights were on, he sounded holier than thou. I wasn't surprised. Well, his lamps are dimmed forever.

Look at how Charlie Rose was destroyed. The old man of sleepy PBS TV was creepy to begin with. I was not surprised that he was groping small girls. The guy did not even respect his age. I could understand if he was dealing with mature and professional women, but interns? And for him to be walking around naked, that's disgusting. He deserved more than a spanking.

Look at Glenn Thrush, Mark Halperin, Lockhart Steele, Michael Oreskes, and so many others. Now they are coming after Tom Brokaw. These are people that you see in suits pontificating as if they are beyond reproach. You lived in Africa, so you must have heard this saying Omarosa told me. It says that there is no anus that you will dig your finger into without touching shit. Men will always be men. I like my men to be men enough to stand their ground.

Do you know why I survived while all these people folded up like pieces of newspapers? Because I am real. I am not fake. I do not present myself as a Pope of some sort. If Bill O'Reilly and Roger Ailes had listened to me, they still would have been around doing what they know how to do best. You don't ever want to appear weak. If you do, they pounce at you. That is the modus operandi of your tribe of condoners of evil.

I am sure that in your quiet moments you see my close similarity with John F. Kennedy, your hero. Like Kennedy, I have refused to accept the world that I have found. I am working hard to change it, from Iran to India. I am busting norms and rearranging alliances. I am shaking things up. You are a nice enough guy to acknowledge that when all your mischievous friends are not around. If you watch me carefully, you will see that over time, I will make politics work again in America. I am scrambling things as a prerequisite to rearranging them. Damn! That was a good one. You can use that expression to describe me. I don't need the credit.

In no time, I will cease to be elusive to your likes. You will then begin to see the hero in me. At that time, I will bring you closer as a token Democrat. I know that you like hanging around the staircase of power. If you like, I can tactically help you accomplish your life goal of becoming a US Senator. If you begin to treat me well, I may even consider having you as my biographer. Best opportunity that you will ever have. You can do for me what you did for Kennedy, Tipper O'Neil, and Reagan. You can be sure that any book with my image and name on the cover is a success. More success than you ever knew.

As someone who has proved beyond any reasonable doubt that I know how the game of politics is played, I can teach you a thing or two. I will tell you what I really think beyond the things I say when I call into *Fox and Friends*. You may become the luckiest member of your despicable class to get the first insight into how I plan to reshape America for the next one thousand years. Really smart ideas.

Write back and let me know what you think about this proposal.

Yours truly,
Donald J. Trump
The 45th President of the United States of America

Donald Trump's Letter to Pope Francis

Sunday, March 25, 2018

Dear Pope Francis,

Your Holiness, how are you doing? The last time we met, your face was gloomy until I stood up to leave. I hope this letter meets you in a better mood. I have forgiven you for spending only twenty-nine minutes with me when you spent over one hour with Obama in 2014. I have asked God to forgive you, for you did not know what you were doing.

Just so you know, after you asked my wife if she fed me their popular Slovenian cake, she ordered one from Uber Eats. Not my kind of cake. I'm perfectly okay with MacDonald's.

You know that I am not your kind of Christian and I do not need anything from your God. But I do think we can work together on a few things. So, stop checking out my Christian credentials. Check out my business credentials and my gut feeling. They are in excellent shape. My trinity is made of me, myself, and I. I cannot be wrong when my conscience is right. On my conscience are etched my ten commandments.

I know you were mad that I pulled out of the climate change agreement. Believe me, it is a hoax. I will get my scientists to reveal the secrets of the fake climate science when you visit me. As for the migrants, we've had enough of those Mexicans. Do you know that they have brought down the average height of Americans? Preposterous. If you like, let Rome take in more Muslims than there are Christians in Italy. When Muslims surround the Vatican and they start bidding to turn Peter's tomb into a mosque, you will understand why I'm fighting for you today.

Like so many men of the cloth like you, I know you do not understand me. I am not fretting about it either. Just like you leave some matters to your God in heaven, I leave some matters to my God, which is history books.

People like you think I'm going too far. As president of the greatest nation in the history of mankind, with the greatest army ever assembled by man, I know there is nothing like going too far. I am the "too far" they are talking about. I decide what is far enough and what is too far. The same way I decide what is classified and what is not.

In simple terms, I don't do sentiments. Believe me, nobody can manipulate me by appealing to my sentimentality. Not me. I see things the way they are, and my first instinct about things has always turned out to be right. It is true, even for projects that I have gone into that failed. Not so many of such, I must say. Even at that, the failure was never my fault.

I'm very tough. I don't bend to extortion by people who think I owe them. I don't owe anyone. I fly with my wings. I don't do favors either, because I don't need favors from people. I only need people to do the right things—half of which is being loyal. And if they fail to do the right thing, I get rid of them.

I don't need men or stones to rise up and praise me. The unprecedented crowd that came to the Washington, DC, Mall at my inauguration can disappear. It won't move me an inch. Unlike losers out there, I don't do this to hear their chants. I do these things because I can hear the chant of yet unwritten history.

I am entitled to one thing and one thing alone—my own stand from which I will try to move the world, just like anybody else. That I am moving the world the farthest of any other president in history is a tribute to my ingenuity. Believe me, the template of my success will be embraced by the generations yet unborn.

The Secret Letters of President Donald J. Trump, Age 72 1/6

If I allow myself to be emotional like all of you, I will cease to be effective. I will join the rest of you in bending over and exposing my backside to those who specialized in drilling into the body to excavate the soul. Pathetic!

It is easy to betray the climate, the angels who escort rain into the clouds and the God who holds the sky in place. What is not easy to betray is our conscience. I will take the knife from friends and enemies, in the front and at the back, but I will never compromise the very thing that makes me, me. You can take that to the bank.

I have a quick question for you. I would have sent it as a tweet, but I know I don't want it to leak out to the press. I will write you a comprehensive letter at a later time.

Since they will not allow me to write "Trump" on the beams of the White House, I need to establish new norms and traditions that will live on when I'm gone. I'm thinking of building a new chimney at the White House when I am reelected president. I'm thinking of gathering the Electoral College people in a room that night for them to cast the vote. Can I please send an aide to come to the Vatican City to understudy the history and tradition of the chimney at the Vatican where smoke gushes out with the election of a new pope?

I am seriously thinking of my next inauguration. I want ten million Americans at the Mall. I want our greatest military in the world to have a parade and display our nuclear weapons for the world to see – and for the world to know not to mess with me. I want the parade to be like the Eucharist of our politics. If you could convince your feeble-minded followers for two thousand years that the Eucharist is the body and blood of that Jewish guy, I can convince Americans that the parade is the artery of our nation.

I had this dream where I was in a toga, like a Roman emperor with a crown on my head. As I was inspecting a parade, Mike Pence stabbed me in the back and ran into the White House. Pope, pray for Pence. Remind him that I am not as naïve as Caesar and he is not as smart as Brutus.

My whole life I have always believed that if one must think, why not think big? If you allow me to send an aide to study your smoke chimney, I can use that opportunity to send Michael Cohen out of the country on a special assignment to the Vatican.

If you do this for me, I will ask my wife's parents to cook *potica*, your favorite Slovenian dessert, for you.

I await your discreet response.

Yours truly,
Donald J. Trump
The 45th President of the United States

Donald Trump's Letter to God

Thursday, April 5, 2018

Dear God,

I'm Donald J. Trump. I guess you know already, but just in case you do not know, I am the 45th president of the United States of America. Okay, I'm just messing around. I know that you are fully aware of who I am. After all, all TV channels in heaven are talking about me just the same way they are doing on Earth. Humongous, isn't it? I am a ratings bonanza for them here on Earth. And I believe it must be the same thing there in heaven.

Come to think of it, maybe I should ask the Pew people to conduct a poll. I bet you, I will come out more popular than you, at least here on Earth. When I get there, I will also give you a run for your money. Terrific run! Mind you, I am not in any rush to get there. So, don't start getting any ideas, buddy.

I would have preferred to send you a tweet, but you don't have a verified Twitter account. Let me tell you, for a man of your status, that is a total disgrace, if you ask me. How do you clap back at your enemies, the Nancy Pelosi, the Obamas, and the Clintons, without a Twitter account? How? I don't get it. Very disappointing!

Anyway, that is not why I am writing you today. God, I have never asked you for anything. Have I? I have never asked you for forgiveness. I don't apologize for anything. So, you should be excited that I am coming to you today with the best deal ever.

My friend pastor John Hagee said that if I moved the US Embassy in Israel from Tel Aviv to Jerusalem that you would do anything I ask you to do. I didn't believe it at first. Then, the other night, you appeared in my dream and asked me to ask for anything, that you would grant it. It told me you were ready to strike a deal. I will now lay out for you the deal.

I am sure you saw me going to church on Easter day. You know I wasn't there to show reverence to you or to your son, Jesus. Forget about his mother—I place all women where they belong—on a different floor from mine. My people said the optics of me going to church was good politics, so I did that. It keeps my poorly educated followers very happy. Just like your followers who are deplorable. I mean, it is the only thing that I agree on with Crooked Hillary Clinton, even though I must not say so in public.

I write to you because the other day, upon my request, my generals showed me what our nuclear arsenals could do. You would not believe this. Do you know that I have the power to wipe out your prized creation, Earth, in just thirty seconds? All I need to do is to wait for the absence of General Kelly, maybe when he is in the toilet. Then I will grab the box containing the nuclear codes. Once I press some buttons (I have them written on my thighs), voilà! North Korea, China, and Russia are off the map of the world. Wait, did I say Russia? That was a mistake.

Last time I checked, I do not have a Trump Tower that I built with my own money in any of those countries. This power to destroy the world is very intoxicating. I wonder how you feel knowing that you have similar powers as I do. I guess the difference is that unlike me, you don't have Congress to explain your actions to. You don't have those unpatriotic knucklehead Democrats flexing their filibuster threat.

My question for you is this: if you had not destroyed the world in Noah's time, do you think that people would have this respect that they have for you now? I don't think so. That is why I am thinking of wiping two or three countries off the face of this earth, and right there I would be ranked higher than any other American president ever. Ever! Ever! Ever!

Learning from your action in Lot's country, Sodom and Gomorrah, all that I need to do is to make a case for the attack of those countries. Maybe I should say that they were taking gold showers in those countries on a Sunday morning. I can pull off an easy case against Iran and North Korea. I know Americans will want me to add Russia, their archenemy, to that list, but that is not happening. Putin and I will dominate the world the way Hitler and Mussolini dreamt of. Of course, I won't acknowledge this publicly, or some of those liberal types would lose their minds. If Hitler and Mussolini had won, the whole of the Western world would have become like Germany without those two million Muslims that Angela Merkel allowed in. Total disaster.

While I have your attention, let me ask you... can you reverse time and make me look the way I did when I was in the US Military Academy in New York. Remember? I mean, you should be able to do so, if you truly are the all-powerful God. Do it slowly so that you won't scare Americans. Instead of letting me grow older in the next seven years of my presidency, make me grow younger and younger until I stabilize as that dashing young man women were dying to date. If you do that transformation, I am sure that the American people would be so impressed that they would suspend their constitution and ask me to keep ruling as their president forever.

After all, the Chinese just did that for Xi Jinping, and the Russians just did the same for Vladimir Putin. America would need a strong man like me in power to keep up with those two. Frankly, I can take care of figuring out how to manipulate public opinion to get what I want. My good friend Putin has promised to help. Good guy! The only thing that can stop me is this age thing and growing old. Americans like their presidents young. I am sure you can do it. Whatever you want me to do for you to raise your profile, I will gladly do so. To be honest with you, if you want me to renovate your throne in heaven, I will send my Mexican workers over to take care of that for you.

While you think about my request, can you make that fucking Robert Mueller disappear? He is the worst person that you ever created. I know you can do it. After all, you made the Titanic sink. You can get one of those alien ships that are on America's skyline every night to come down and pick him up and take him to Jupiter where he belongs. I will ask our air force to hold fire until the operation has been successfully completed. Nobody gets hurt. Please drop him in the same Arabian Sea where Obama dropped Osama. Let the same whale that ate Osama eat him. Like I said, nobody gets hurt. If you do that, I promise to name that sea "Trump Sea." Why not? By the way, why is there no sea named after Trump? Long overdue, if you ask me.

I need to enjoy my presidency, you know. I need to put my legs up on the center table and relax. I need to enjoy the Oval Office the same way Bill Clinton did. I am sure Bill was not having fun when Kenneth Starr was all up in his business. Obama wouldn't have brought Stevie Wonder and that thug, Common, to perform in the White House if he had a Mueller after his black ass over his birth certificate or for smoking weed at Columbia University. Believe me, I have held up fine under intense pressure that no president in the history of America has endured. Don't tell me about Nixon. Nixon was a crook; I am sure you know that. Me, I only sell my name to buildings and most probably, my soul to women. Not bad... considering how rich I am. But you are used to that. King David did worse things and you still struck a deal with him and his household that the Jews could have the Star of David on their flag. I want the Star of Trump on the American flag. If I need to make a sacrifice to redeem myself, I am willing to sacrifice any of my children, with the exception of Ivanka.

I don't want to be selfish, my guy. If you need me to take care of anything for you here on Earth, just say so. You know what? You and I can form a partnership. You take care of some things from over there while I take care of some other things over here for you. Trust me, it can help fix your damaged reputation. I can absorb some blame from you while you do the same for me. The stupid amendments to the US Constitution won't let me do some things that I want to do. Bigly frustrating!

Oh, one more thing – about Ivanka. Is there any chance that you can make an exception to the rule? You know the rule that I am talking about. After all, Cain and Abel did something with their siblings or mother or daughter or alien to keep your creation going. My White House doctor, rear admiral Ronny Jackson, told me that genetic sexual attraction (GSA) is a real medical condition. So I am sure that you understand perfectly what I'm going through.

Don't think that I am crazy for raising these issues. You are the one that is considered bipolar or at least schizophrenic. Based on how destructive you are and quick-tempered, I think I am mild in comparison.

My proposal would be a win-win for us. Anyway, I have to go. General Kelly is bringing Melania over to see me.

Yours truly,
Donald J. Trump
The 45th President of the United States of America.

Donald Trump's Letter to Stormy Daniels

Thursday, April 5, 2018

Dear Stormy Daniels,

My name is Donald J. Trump. By the way, I am the 45th president of the United States of America.

I write just to say, fuck you.
Fuck you.
Fuck you.
Fuck you.
Excuse me! Oops, I've done that already.

In case you are wondering why—fuck you for making me look bad. In 2006, you looked okay. Maybe I should say, you looked decent enough then. But now, I don't think so. You look like a horseface. A sad horseface.

After thirty, you should've just checked your fat self out, quietly. But you didn't. So, I fired you the same way I fired that Miss Universe from Venezuela.

Fuck you for not making that distinction. For giving people the impression that I would ever touch a woman like you. Even if I had married you, by the time you had gotten this old with horrible wrinkles all over your face, I would have divorced you. That would be the smart thing to do. If you doubt me, ask my ex-wives, Maria and Ivana. I cannot deal with old layers like you hanging around me. Trust me on that.

Fuck you for putting an image in the minds of my fans that being with you meant that I have technically been with thirteen million other women. I may be bad in math, but I know that calculation too well. You sleep with about sixty men a month. Those sixty men, being in your industry, also sleep with sixty other women in a month. And those sixty other women had also slept with sixty other men. In essence, if you multiply those, 60 x 60 x 60 x 60 x 60, I essentially slept with over thirteen million women by sleeping with you without a condom. What an inordinate amount of diseases that I exposed myself to. Dangerous!

Fuck you for stealing $130,000 from me. Go and ask Mexican workers who work for me, I don't part with such an amount of money for that kind of shitty job you did. My whole life is about making sure I'm not cheated. It's only that I was running for president and I did not want any BS from you. Otherwise, I wouldn't have asked my lawyer, Michael, to pay you a penny. You don't even know how to spank a man – a basic requirement of your career. Such a disgrace! If you want to learn, go to Russia and learn from the best.

Nonsense!

I knew you were a Democrat. Pornography is to Democrats what Sunday Mass is to the family-friendly Republicans. I'm sure Schumer and Pelosi put you up to this. It is another plot by the deep state to impeach a president they do not like.

Fuck you for bastardizing my "Make America Great Again" slogan to "Make America Horny Again." Big-league theft!

Fuck you.
Fuck you.
Fuck you.
Excuse me! Oops, I did that already.

Yours truly,
Donald J. Trump
The 45th President of the United States

Donald Trump's Letter to Dr. Martin Luther King Jr.

Friday, April 6, 2018

Dear Dr. Martin Luther King Jr.,

How are you, man? Bored with channel flipping, I went on YouTube and saw this old clip of yours. I just finished watching the old footage of an interview you had with Fake NBC news. In the interview, you were talking of black folks having a disadvantage because they were given nothing after slavery. You were ranting about how white folks were given American land in the Midwest and in the West. You talked as if we did not know what happened when Robert Mugabe of Zimbabwe gave black folks land that he stole from white farmers. We knew what happened. They did not know what to do with the land. They let it go to waste. Unbelievable. So why do you think it would have been any different if America had given land to black folks?

    What are we even talking about? We have tried it. Look at the historical black colleges. We gave them to you guys to run. What happened? You ran them into the ground. Losers! And you people turned around and came to the White House with hats in hand begging for handouts. Meanwhile, when I try to get them to answer, "Who is your daddy?" they are too pompous to say, "Donald J. Trump."

Even to find one of your fine women and give her to me, they won't. I am sure you know that I won't mind having one of your luscious ladies—not the second-class poorly endowed type like Lupita Nyong'o. When I was free to hunt, they kept saying no, even with my money. They do not want my kind of white man. As if there was not a time that I looked like George Clooney. Have you seen my New York Military Academy pictures?

Wasn't it in *The Wolf of Wall Street* that a character said that black women taste sexually different? If I remember correctly, it said black women taste like Jamaican sugar. I used to crave for such, but not anymore. Seeing me around them would destroy my reputation with the owners of this country. Have you tasted white women? Did you ask her while you were doing it if she had a dream that one day she would be moaning beneath a black man?

I feel we would have gotten along considering that you liked women just like me. But you were just too poor to come near my circle. But you eventually did well for yourself. Knowing where you came from, your achievement was huge. People say what happened to you was horrible. But I don't think so. You have a holiday named after you. So far, I don't see Democrats doing that for me. I have Mitch McConnell in my armpit. I could make his wife Secretary of Happiness and he would carve out a holiday in my name. The only obstacle in my path is the stupid filibuster rule in the Senate.

Another way to look at it is that, if you were still alive, you would have become like an older version of Jesse Jackson or Al Sharpton. Have you seen Al of late? He looks like those beef jerky sticks from Jamaica or the dry meats from Africa. As for Jesse Jackson, I think he has diabetes, or is it Parkinson's disease? Maybe you would have caught HIV or AIDS. Granted, the great American health system that Obama wanted to destroy with his Obamacare would have kept you alive just like it kept Magic Johnson alive. But who wants to live that kind of life, popping pills day and night? I have left instructions with my doctors: any day that my health is no longer tremendously excellent, 100 percent, they should quietly end it. My will has been written. Everything is all set. Don Jr. is up for the surprise of his life.

By the way, did you hear that I have brought black unemployment to its lowest level since recorded history? Did you hear that? I didn't do it by giving out food stamps and other handouts to your people in the inner cities. I did it by being a role model for them. You talked of America demanding that black people pull themselves up by their bootstraps. Why not? Your excuse is that America is asking people who had no boots to pull themselves up by the straps.

In case you have forgotten, my grandfather came here with nothing. He worked his ass off to establish the little things my father built on. With nothing but sheer genius, I have built on that little beginning to the place where I am on top of the world's most historical individuals. I am no longer in a fight with the rich guys on who is richer. I have since left that to them and *Forbes* magazine. The only question left unanswered now is whether my image should be carved on Mount Rushmore with the great presidents or whether a new gigantic one should be carved on a brand-new mountain. One of my people said I should consider a new mountain that emerged on Virginia Beach called Mount Trashmore. I will go and check it out as soon as I am done with this Mueller nonsense and I set my mind on building the Donald Trump Presidential Library. It would be sited at the original campus of Trump University. Rudy Giuliani is working on those tiny details. My job is to come and cut the red tape.

I am sure that I have taken a lot of your time. But before I go, I want to let you know that I had the privilege of looking at your FBI files the other day. That is one perk of being president and having your own handpicked FBI guys, not those leftover Obama moles. Anyway, so you were quite a stud, my friend. Without money, you got the church going, Bible-carrying women to fight for space on your bed. And by the way, I saw the white women too. Nice taste you had, I must say. How did you do that? You should have written a best-selling book on that topic, if not that, unfortunately, you got shot.

The Secret Letters of President Donald J. Trump, Age 72

By now, I know that your wound must have healed, but the wound of this nation has not. Even after my white folks elected one of your people president, black folks are not yet satisfied. I don't know what more your people want. I was the only one screaming that the guy was born in Kenya, but your folks did not support me. Eight years after, he was disgraced out of office as I kicked him and his handpicked successor out. Now black people knew the man did nothing for them. Knowing how sneaky he was, he probably did more for his home country of Kenya than the inner city of Chicago where five hundred young black men are killed each year.

It may interest you to know my solution to that horrific killing field called Chicago. I said that every child old enough to hold his or her mother's breast should be taught how to shoot a gun. Bad gunmen thrive simply because good kids are not armed. Give every black kid on the street of Chicago a gun, and the bad guys will know that they do not have a monopoly of violence anymore. And they will chill. That is exactly what I do to bullies, using my Twitter account. I knock them to size and to the shape that I want. If you doubt me, ask Jeff Sessions. I am sure he was a senator when you were making your "I Have a Dream" speech.

Trust me, Mississippi is no longer burning. It is now a hub for alternative facts.

Let me tell you what some of your overpaid brothers whose sole job was to entertain us on the football field did recently. They followed that crazy boy Colin Kaepernick to disrespect our national anthem. They said they were protesting the killing of black thugs by the police. Disgusting waste of brain. But trust me, I got the job done. I went on my bully pulpit. I told my fellow rich white people who owned the sports teams to fire those sons of bitches. Knowing that they would go broke in less than one year after leaving their professional leagues, nobody told them to shape up quickly.

As you can see, I am taking care of my white nationalists who discovered this country, own it and built it. I know what you are thinking now. That it is the sweat of black folks that built this country. Wrong! It is the brain that designed the structure that truly built it. Not the ordinary labor that machines and animals could do. Do you understand? If you guys were the ones who built this country, why haven't your people transformed the inner cities? Why? Who is stopping you from building a replica of the White House in Harlem? Answer me.

I am not very sure that you know me. I am the billionaire whose life is the model of that '80s movie *Pretty Woman*, remember? Trust me, you are not my first choice of a leader. You are kind of a sissy. Malcolm X is my kind of leader. He is fierce and not intimidated. He was also not interested in the direction the wind blows. But during your time, you overshadowed him. Not anymore. This is Trump's time. Hm. I need to get Ivanka to trademark Trump's Time for me.

One last thing – did you hear that my "America First" speech now has more views than your "I Have a Dream" speech?

I just thought you would like to know that. All the best. When I win a Nobel Prize for Peace, I will write you again.

Yours truly,
Donald J. Trump
The 45th President of the United States of America

Donald Trump's Letter to Vladimir Putin

Friday, April 13, 2018

My buddy Putin,

Thank you for giving me the permission to mention your name in my tweet. It was clear proof that our back channel is working. Is my Jewish in-law, Jared, a genius or what? It fooled a lot of them. One called me to say that it was good to see the Donald getting his balls back. I have always had my balls. They might have been spanked here and there, splashed with golden shower mixed with holy water by daughters of Eve, but all and all, they are intact all the time and ever ready to spring into action when needed.

You know, we should do more of this. You give me the free hand to do some of those things that American presidents do to feel presidential. Things that do not make sense. Like firing a few Tomahawk missiles here and there, call you names while at the same time nothing changes fundamentally. I love that. One day, though, I hope someone will explain to me why we look away when hundreds of thousands of people die but make all the noise when sixty people die from a chemical weapon.

What we do is similar to what my grandmother and grandfather did during the days of their secret love affairs. My mother used to tell me of how my grandmother was a member of a church choir and her boyfriend, my grandfather, was a choirmaster. Each time my grandmother was late for choir practice, my grandfather would punish her severely for coming late. That way he covered up their love affair. Genius!

If you ask me, you can even shoot down one or two of our missiles over Syria. It only costs $2 million apiece. We have a stockpile of over 3,500 Tomahawk missiles looking for a war to deploy them. Do you know that we keep increasing our military budget each year, buying equipment that even our military is telling us that they don't need anymore just to keep our vast military-industrial complex going?

In your own case, I guess you are the Russian industrial complex yourself. You and your friends and family determine what to build and who to build it. You don't answer to any senator or useless FBI people. Imagine! My own Justice Department ordering a search of my attorney's offices without giving me a heads-up. Why did I appoint them? Why do I pay them? Can you believe it? Do I need to do an intervention in my Justice Department before they protect my interest? Do I have to do to them what you are doing in Ukraine? Or do I have to go the whole way and annex the unpatriotic bunch of people the way you annexed Crimea? I know why government sucks. I know why – nobody knows what they should be doing much less how they should do it. This kind of nonsense does not happen in the Trump Organization. Never!

So, my buddy, when are you going to visit me in Mar-a-Lago, Florida? I have a very nice place there. Though it is not as nice as your posh $1B secret hideout in Praskoveevka off the coast of the Black Sea. The CIA showed me pictures. I could not believe that you have your own casino in that place and four heliports. What I don't understand is why you also need a church inside the place. Come on! Didn't you hear that the pope recently confirmed what I have always believed—that there is no hell? You have quite good taste, I must say. But if you let me visit, I can show you a few finishing touches that you can add to it that would make it all the more exquisite. Trust me.

Oh, I have a small request to make. Would it be possible for you to announce that Russian women don't pee on themselves for others to watch? It would help Melania to calm down a bit. She thinks there is a 1 percent chance that such a thing happens in Russia. Such a rumor destroys the reputation of all the beautiful girls that Russia is endowed with. As someone who has been privileged to be in the midst of these heavenly beauties, it hurts me to know that some scrupulous hypocritical people have these images of Russian women in their dirty minds. It would be a PR win for Russia if you come out and deny the possibility of such in Moscow, where you don't even let gay people display their disgusting lifestyle. You and I are in locked steps about that one. It is just that the liberals in America have gone so far with their madness that I cannot put the genie back into the box. Otherwise…

Don't worry about the part about hookers in my hotel. Every country has its hookers. And sometimes, you never know who a hooker is, you know. Some smart men, with a single look, turn decent women into hookers. I think it was Dominique Strauss-Kahn, a lawyer who once said, "I defy you to tell the difference between a nude prostitute and a nude classy woman." Some hookers don't even know that they are hookers. Even if someone finally shows the world a picture of the Donald and some loose women in Moscow, I can explain it away. After all, we all have been around women that we had no idea were hookers.

Let me ask you, how do you handle people who do not abide by agreements not to disclose things? It is an epidemic here in America. People's words do not mean a thing anymore. Not even threats to have them pay $1million. I fear that the American society will collapse if there is no way to keep people from spilling all they know. I know you have mastered that act. Wonderful job you did in Britain. Please, when you reply to my letter, could you shed more light onto how you sealed the mouths of despicable slimeballs in Russia? Maybe my last letter to you wasn't detailed enough, or maybe something was lost in translation.

I don't even want to talk about loyalty. That tested ancient value is dead in America. People just open their mouths and say anything without consequences. In public, I condemned what you did to those untruthful former KGB slime balls of yours in England, but you know that I understand. Our whole Western society will collapse if things that happened at the Moscow Ritz-Carlton cannot stay at Moscow Ritz-Carlton. If every conversation that took place in Air Force One or the White House is made public, we might as well turn off the lights and shut down the republic. I don't know why all these weak-minded people in my country could not get it. I wished I were president in the '60s when John F. Kennedy could bring Marilyn Monroe to the White House and everyone would look the other way. These days, there are so many fake news people hanging around. You put them in their place so well in Russia that I want you to share some of your secrets with me. Please, when you have the time, do that for me, or else I may snap one day. You may hear that I walked into that White House briefing room, opened my zipper, and peed on all of them so that they really would have something to write about.

If for any reason I leave office before you, please assure me that no matter what the next president of the United States does for you, you will never reveal what happened between us. For the sake of my Ivanka, my Ivanka, please seal it for another seventy years after my death. I know you vowed that you are going to your grave with them, but you know how old age often makes someone start to rethink certain things. As for me, you have nothing to fear from my end.

How is our November midterm election looking like from your end? I am counting on you. The polls here do not look good. But I am sure that if you won reelection by 76 percent, you could make my party at least retain control of the House of Representatives. It is the only way I can avoid impeachment.

You know, sometimes I wish I did not marry again after my second divorce. I wish I could be like you, free and outgoing without anyone looking at me the way my vice president often looks at me when I am shaking the hands of beautiful women. All these church people have a way of making someone feel guilty. Maybe I should get a cross and wear it around my neck all the time, like you do, so that Mike Pence will stop looking at me with suspicion.

Or maybe I should get a dog. What do you think? Maybe it will soften my image and make these liberals get off me a bit. It is just that those animals stink. Also, I always feel that they are for low-class people. I have expensive carpets, and those animals pee all over the place, even those that are well-groomed. But I think it has done you some good in softening your image. Maybe we should arrange for you to give me a dog when I visit Moscow in the near future. That would be a symbol of a new relationship between our two great countries. Who knows, it may rub off on me some of your great leadership skills that I greatly admire.

Until next time.

Your friend,
Donald J. Trump
The 45th President of the United States of America

Donald Trump's Letter to Allah

Wednesday, April 19, 2018

Dear Allah,

I swear to God, I don't know if you are God or not. My gut tells me that you are something else… like a kind of substitute God. I am just being honest with you. And as you can imagine, that is one hell of a difficult thing for me to be.

Are you God that answers to another name? Why do I even care? It doesn't matter so much. I would have written your son, Muhammad, sorry, I mean, your prophet, but his worshippers, sorry, I mean, his followers, get angry so quickly at the slightest mention of his name. They particularly get mad if anyone mentions his name without putting "peace be unto him." I don't get it. But what business is it of mine?

Do you ever talk to the Christian God? Do you guys ever have a meeting of the Gods? How do you do this job? How do you decide where to intervene and where not to? Do you think of the poverty that is perpetuated by those who fervently carry your book, the Koran, and the book of the Christian God, the Bible?

I understand that unlike the Christian God, you don't have a son. Which makes perfect sense, because if you have a son, it follows that you have a wife, or at least a baby mama. The first means that you have some annoying in-laws while the later means you have to deal with your baby mama's obnoxious girlfriends who tell her all that is wrong with you and how to put you in your place. I have been there. That was why I decided to hire Michael Cohen to fix such inconveniences for me. I asked him to spend as much as a cool million dollars if necessary.

I don't care who you are, even as a billionaire, I still have to deal with those annoying matters. I think it is the same thing with all you gods. So, it is a smart move on your part not to have a son. If you ask me, whenever you want to have a baby, go for a daughter. They are easier to raise, and they have greater loyalty to their father than sons.

I think if you want to surpass the Christian God in a jiffy, you should have a daughter as soon as possible. A daughter as tall and beautiful as my classy Ivanka will do you good. When you have her, send her to Pakistan or India. Let her be persecuted and killed like Benazir Bhutto. She was a piece of ass when she was young. If Malala Yousafzai was given the Nobel Peace Prize for being shot, women would worship your daughter at this point in history.

But then again, you need a son to inherit your name. Daughters, you can love them to pieces, but they can still end up marrying Jews. Imagine if Muhammad had a daughter that he loved and she decided that she would marry a Jew. How would Muhammad feel about that? Despite my wisdom, I wouldn't have stomached it if not for the fact that my son-in-law is rich, in real estate, and understands the back channels of New York City business.

Forget all these preliminary talks. Let me go straight to why I am writing. You see, your worshippers are one nuclear bomb away from destroying the world. I don't know how long we have before they get it. They are already calling the bomb in Pakistan, Allah's own bomb. Who knows how long we can keep one of those from the hands of your bad children determined to kill us all? During dinner one day, Stephen Miller told me that another Saudi prince could go rogue again. But this time, instead of carrying his wealth into the mountains of Afghanistan, he may just use it to buy the bomb from Pakistan or a crazy country like North Korea. If that happens, we are screwed.

    I write to let you know that it is not necessary. Please tell your worshippers that it is not. They have won. Anything drastic from them would be just overkill. Without firing one shot, your worshippers have taken over Europe from Britain to France. The fate of Europe was finally sealed when Germany let in two million Muslims from Syria, Iraq, and Afghanistan. In another two hundred years from now, the Emir of London and the Emir of Rome will be taking the wealth of Europe to Mecca. Stephen said that was how Mansa Musa liquidated Africa.

    Out in public, I won't accept this, but I can confide in you that it is a hopeless situation for us. It is similar to the fight I'm having with those Mexicans. Even if I build a wall and don't let any one of them come into America anymore, we are already screwed. The number that are in already are having babies like rabbits, such that in another one hundred years, they will have taken over the land we took from them in wars, without firing a shot. Even if Europe does not let another Muslim in, those in, like our Mexicans and other Latinos, are already having enough babies to take over.

    So you might as well tell your foot soldiers to chill. There is no need to burn down the London Bridge when they can mount the crescent on top of it in a short while without any opposition. The same goes for the Eiffel Tower in Paris. It is all theirs if only they have patience. The way they are taking over churches from Europeans who do not go to church anymore and turning them into mosques is the same way they will take over all the monuments therein. In as little as two hundred years from now, the Vatican may become the official residence of the Sultan of Rome. The grave of St. Peter will be turned into another pit where Muslim's faithful, too old to go to Medina, will go and stone the devil.

    While you communicate with them, Allah please, you need to pick someone amongst them who will lead a reform within Islam. You know the way Martin Luther reformed Christianity. The way the Bible's Old Testament has in it enough provisions to chop off heads, but modern Christians pretend that it does not exist.

Though I wish I could chop off the heads of some fake news peddlers. Without moderation, Islam will destroy itself. And because Christianity is already packing up, we need to have a reformed Islam just in case it is the only religion we on Earth are left with. So, think about updating the Koran. It has been a while since someone looked at it.

All the best handling those monsters that you have unleashed on the world. But I will tell you what Pompeo told me. He said, "Muslims' silence in the face of extremism coming from the best-funded Islamic advocacy organizations and many mosques across America is absolutely deafening. It casts doubt upon the commitment to peace among adherents of the Muslim faith." He also said, "It has made these Islamic leaders across America potentially complicit in these acts of terrorism." The guy is a smart man. When he is not bullshitting just for political purposes, he thinks just like me. I love him.

If any Islamic terrorism act happens again in America, I will make all Muslims prove that they are good Muslims by not criticizing America. If they do, I won't think twice before I lock them up, all Muslims. So, you better warn your folks. My national security advisor, John Bolton, said that the virus of Wahhabism has infiltrated my America. And that was how some of our white boys learned how to shoot kids studying in school. They learned it from your boys. Our white boys learned terrorism from your boys since the days of Yasser Arafat. That is a total disaster.

It is up to you do something about this.

It will surprise you to know that I am reading a book on how the Spanish expelled Muslims from their land in the seventeenth century. I don't remember the book's title now, but I am getting hints. It is never too late. We can reverse this trend. Insha Allah.

Yours truly,
Donald J. Trump
The 45th President of the United States of America

Donald Trump's Letter to Michael Cohen

Thursday, April 19, 2018

To Michael Cohen:

Micoo, you fucked up, big time. You really fucked up. This is not *The Sopranos*. This is for real. Moron! Damn!

How could you not know that they could raid your law office and your hotel room? What kind of law school did you go to? So much for Jewish lawyers being the best there is. I should have known when you were driving a Porsche in college that you were not paying attention to what you were being taught. Stupid! Next time, I'm getting a lawyer who went to Harvard.

If I did not ask you of the possibilities of that happening, I would not be this mad. But you assured me that it would not happen. You said that these documents would never be made public. And I trusted you. You said that the US Constitution protected and guaranteed lawyer-client privilege. So, what happened? Were you reading your own constitution upside down?

How could you not know there were exceptions? You screwed up. You screwed yourself up. You want to make me look bad, but I won't let you. It so happens that even New York City taxi drivers driving with your medallions know this about the limits of lawyer-client privilege.

I should have known that you are not that smart when you used the email of my Trump Organization to negotiate the nondisclosure agreement with that woman. Also, I made you a millionaire, yet you had the effrontery to go about complaining to low-lives that you hang out with that I had not reimbursed you the $130,000 that you gave that woman. Imagine! You were collecting dirty dollar bills from taxi drivers when I picked you up from that gutter and made you a millionaire.

That aside, I'm disappointed that when the crooked FBI boys came to your doorstep, you folded up. What kind of a pit bull does something like that? Whatever happened to your often-quoted pledge of eternal loyalty? "If somebody does something Mr. Trump doesn't like, I do everything in my power to resolve it to Mr. Trump's benefit. If you do something wrong, I'm going to come at you, grab you by the neck, and I'm not going to let you go until I'm finished."

What happened? You just saw a few FBI officers and you peed in your pants. Disgusting! All you needed to do was to pick up the phone and call me. You did not do that. That is really fucked up.

I could have rumpled the search warrant and thrown it into the trash can. I could have sent the CIA to storm your hotel room and law offices and have them disarm the FBI. I could have sent the NIA to storm in immediately afterward and disarm the CIA. I could have sent the MIA to storm in next and disarm the NIA. By the end of the day, nobody ever would know who had the documents.

You really messed up. But I won't let you mess me up. If your intention is to inflict emotional distress on me, it won't work. Never!

What happened in New York City won't happen in Putin's Moscow. What happened in Manhattan won't happen in Xi Jinping's Beijing. Why, then, should it happen in Trump's America?

It is all your fault!

America, in our own eyes, is becoming a shithole country. Under this condition, who wants to be the commander-in-chief of the armed forces? Fuck that.

I want to be the commander-in-chief of the New York City police. I want to be the commander-in-chief of the FBI.

When this is all over, I will demand those additional titles to that of the commander-in-chief of the armed forces. If I have to give up being the commander-in-chief of the coast guard to get command of the FBI, I will do so in a heartbeat. Fuck the coast guard.

Micco, I'm good at this. I will persevere. I thrive under pressure. You will see. America will soon have a reason to proclaim the categorical recognition of my genius. It is long overdue. It will blow all the naysayers away.

All that I ask you is not to crumble under pressure. There is no boundary to the options in front of me. People talk of pardoning you; that is the simplest option I have. But I did not make my name by doing simple things, going after low-hanging fruits. I made my name by tackling the big things, blowing up paths where bushes were before. I will use this case as another terrific teaching moment for Americans.

I hear those lazy talking heads talk about how I break the American norms. Tremendous knuckleheads they must be. By the time I am done with America, it will have become clear to them that I am the norms they were talking about.

So, my friend, do not fear. How did Kendrick Lamar say it? I am the butterfly that does not need pimping.

Stay strong. I will write you again.

I won't call you for a while because I have been told that you could be wearing a wire to record me confessing to crimes of some sort. You know that I am not stupid. When they approach you for that with a promise of a reduced sentence, tell them that my nuclear button and my pardon button are bigger than theirs.

My buddy, you really fucked up. But don't worry, big daddy will clean it up. I will not let any personal injury happen to you.

Yours truly,
Donald J. Trump (a.k.a. David Dennison)
The 45th President of the United States of America

Donald Trump's Letter to Nelson Mandela

Monday, April 16, 2018

Hello Mr. Mandela,

Sorry on the death of your ex-wife, Winnie Mandela. If I had wanted to be presidential, I would have said that Melania and I have your family in our thoughts and prayers. But that would give an impression that Melania's thoughts and my thoughts are anywhere close. Also, some people may assume that we are one of those traditional American families that sit at one dinner table to eat or kneel down to pray before going to bed. Wrong! We don't do things like that. If there is any kind of supplication going on, it is coming from Melania toward me. Believe me, the bigger truth is that we don't give a hoot what happens to you guys in that Dark Continent.

I once said in one of those candid moments at the White House that you all are from shithole countries. Your people and your liberal allies, who do not like to hear the truth, went ballistic. Huge hullabaloo erupted. I didn't get it. Please explain to me—where in that continent is there a glimmer of light? Is it the big-for-nothing giant, Nigeria? Is it the Islamist infested Egypt? Or it is the Portuguese colony of Angola? Just tell me. Even the midlevel countries like Kenya and Uganda cannot tell their right from their left after fifty years of independence. Which tells me that the footing of these nations is faulty.

In fact, I think the premise that you Africans are mature enough to govern yourself is up for debate. Sad! I know people like you may not like to hear straight talk like this, but it is the truth. Look at Zimbabwe. It was doing very well when white people were running the country. Mugabe and his group of thugs said they were the majority and that the majority should rule. Thirty years after, Zimbabwe went to the dogs. The same thing is happening to your beloved South Africa. If not for your people getting rid of Jacob Zuma, South Africa was less than a dozen years away from becoming another Zimbabwe.

Until your wife died, I could not figure out what was wrong with you all. Now I know. Africa lacks people like me. It is incredible. You people lack smart men of integrity who are willing to put Africa first. That was where you sucked. You were too accommodating, like American Democrats. It is always leading to total disaster. You keep giving and keep giving to make everyone feel good, until you turn a nation of men into a formless mash of weak-hearted individuals that stand on nothing.

Believe me, you don't treat white men with kids' gloves. It doesn't work. I don't acknowledge something like this in public, but I can say it in this secret letter. If we start developing soft bleeding hearts like you did in prison, we will one day call back what remains of Native Americans and hand Manhattan back to them. But we have them confined to whatever reservations they are in, build casinos for them, make sure there are sufficient alcohol and drugs for them. That way, we don't have to worry about them waking up to ask how they lost their country. Instead, they wake up to inject themselves with insulin, take 40 milligrams of Prozac, and pray to what remains of their mountains and their rivers just to see tomorrow. Those who do not get the answer they want either commit suicide or contract tuberculosis just for the fun of getting the United States government's assistance.

It is the same thing with your cousins here—African Americans. If we start having pity for them, acknowledging that they really did the manual labor that built America, it would embolden them. Losers. You will hear them scream that they need reparations for slavery and all that. You can see what we tell them when they raise matters like that. We say, hey, your fore-parents lived rent-free and were fed at the cost of the slave masters. The slave masters even provided security for them. That way, we shut them up.

The point that I am making is that if you had put South African blacks first, you would have given economic empowerment to them. But you didn't. I just did not have Africa on my radar then. Otherwise, I would have come down there and helped you guys build some high-rise buildings to get your black folks out of shanty towns into modern buildings with toilets and bathrooms. As a result, your country went on a total free fall.

Winnie wanted to do that, including giving them land to farm. I don't know about giving them land though. Your people in Uganda and Zimbabwe who received and occupied white-owned lands didn't know what to do with them. Instead of giving them land, I would build sports facilities for them, put in music studios in their neighborhoods. I think your people can do well singing and dancing, running around a field pursuing any kind of ball the white man throws out there. Big deal! You guys are good at entertaining the rich white folks like me, so you might as well have what you need to excel in that inconsequential aspect of life.

So let me ask you again, why don't you people allow the likes of your ex-wife to lead? You need people that would put Africa first. Whoever is stopping that from happening is not your friend. Some of my people in the White House told me you had someone like that in the person of Patrice Lumumba in Congo. What happened to him? Whoever stopped him from accomplishing his mission is the real enemy of the African people. I know what I am saying. The same kinds of losers are trying to stop me from accomplishing the work that I am determined to do for America.

I was told that while you were in Robben Prison worrying about wearing shorts instead of long pants, Winnie was in the battlefield of South Africa attending funerals of your dead activists and comrades. You can see why you came out soft while she remained strong and committed to the cause till the end. This is what I honestly believe: you cannot have mission accomplished if you are not ready to accomplish it by any means necessary. That was how I won the US presidential election that nobody believed that I would win, not even Melania. I did it all by myself and in my own way.

Anyway, I am thinking that after winning my second term in office, I should establish a Truth and Reconciliation Commission to look into Clinton's Vincent Forster, Obama's Birth Certificate, Crooked Hillary's Benghazi, and Slime James Comey's high crimes. I want them tried for sedition in a Rivona kind of dramatic way if they do not come to the commission to confess their sins. I want to personally assign James Comey his prison number. I have already made up my mind on what it would be. In a satirical way, I have decided to order the prison chief to give him your 46664 prison number. He is the kind of man that brought apartheid to your beautiful country. Just take a look at him. Doesn't he look like P. W. Botha?

I have seen women from your country: Charlize Theron, Sasha Pieterse, and Lesley-Ann Brandt in Hollywood. I'm very much impressed! I think there may be more of their type where they came from. Maybe when I retire from the presidency in 2028, I will visit South Africa. My only fear is the HIV/AIDs that you guys have over there. I hope by then your HIV/AIDS epidemic is under control. I don't want to take any risk, you know. If what happened at the penthouse of Moscow's Ritz-Carlton happens in Johannesburg's Ritz-Carlton, your countryman, Trevor Noah, would have an orgasm on air.

Okay, I have to go. This place sucks sometimes. John Kelly is knocking at the door. Who knows, it may be time to fire someone again.

Yours truly,
Donald J. Trump
The 45th President of the United States

Donald Trump's Letter to Barack Obama

Sunday, April 22, 2018

Dear Barack,

I saw you making my wife laugh out loud at Barbara Bush's funeral. I did not like it at all. She has not laughed out loud with me since she took in with our son, Barron. In all of my quarrels with you, I have never taken it out on your chimpanzee lookalike wife. I actually drafted a tweet to send out, tagging you, but I changed my mind. I knew you would not be courageous enough to respond. At best, you would run to your Hollywood comedy friends to give you something to say as a clapback.

I write to ask you to desist from going near my wife. No matter the temptation, do not try to talk to her when next you see her. If she talks to you, just ignore her. She is used to that. I do that all the time. If you fail to follow this simple rule, I may be forced to reveal the things I found in your FBI files. So, don't try me. Believe me, I won't say this again.

Imagine the cold shoulders I got from her because of you. I don't know what silly idea you put into her little brain that she came back acting puffed up. Maybe it is one of those little silly things you tell your Kool-Aid drinking crowd of simple-minded people. I worked hard to get her where I wanted her to be—a place where she knows very little but feels that she knows a lot. Do not mess it up for me.

I even heard that you recommended a book to her. And she actually bought the book and started to read it. What does she look like to you? A bimbo from Las Vegas or Novo Mesto? Mind your own business. You won't be happy if I recommend a plastic surgeon to Michelle. Or don't you think that her arms need to be trimmed to make her look like a woman? Don't get me started. You don't want to find out what extremes I will take if you stay on this current path.

Anyway, this is not why I am writing you today. As you can see, I have solved what you said would be the biggest challenge of my presidency, without raising a finger. I just used my incredible bully pulpit. It is something that was available to you, but you failed to use it. Shame, shame, shame. I hope you will be honest enough to call a world press conference and tell the world that I am the greatest president that ever existed in the 242-year history of these United States.

I am not holding my breath. If the Nobel Prize were like the Grammy Awards, I would have loved to see you come on stage and hand me the 2018 Nobel Prize for Peace. But to think of it, you giving that honor to me would be cheapening it. Yours was a token affirmative action kind of Nobel Prize. Even you acknowledged that you did not deserve it. If you had any iota of integrity in you, you should have returned it to the Nobel Committee after eight years as the president of the United States without making an inch of improvement in world peace. You failed in the Middle East. You failed in Libya. You failed even in your home country, Kenya. Unbelievable!

You couldn't even issue a green card to your uncle. This was a man whose house you squatted while you attended Harvard. You watched him get deported like your sick auntie. Pathetic. And you were supposed to be a lawyer. How smart were you, dear affirmative action lawyer? I got a green card for my ungrateful Melania and her parents. Nothing difficult there.

I singlehandedly unified North and South Korea without firing any weapon. I did not even sit down at a summit to accomplish it. I just showed my big nuclear buttons and my large thumbnail ready to press the button, and the Rocket Man knew that his game was up. While you were busy trying to appear presidential, I simply did it the way we do business in the New York real estate world. If you had any honor left in you, you should be screaming to the hearing of anyone in the world that I am a genius. You should be tweeting that nobody has done this job of being the president of the United States of America better than me.

It is good that we have not talked since you handed power over to me. And I want it to remain that way. In any case, there is nothing to talk about with a featherweight like you. When I am done wiping out your toxic footprints from the landscape of America, then I will declare to my fellow Americans that our nightmare is finally over. Maybe then I will consider pardoning you for the series of cons you perpetuated on our United States of America.

If questions about who you were forced you to consume alcohol, smoke marijuana, and do cocaine in your teenage years, I wonder what you will smoke when I reveal all the cons you have perpetuated in America, starting from your immaculate conception to your birth in a manger in Nyang'oma Kogelo, Kenya. Don't think I don't know. Maybe you will embrace opioids then.

I also know what you did when you visited Pakistan and India in 1981. And guess what? I know things that you did in the '80s with your little live-in Asian girlfriend, Sheila—things that your ever-trusting Michelle does not even know. As for Rev. Jeremiah Wright, your pastor that you threw under the bus for your vain presidential ambition, I am in possession of some stories. I have news for you. I know some terrible things about you and him that you do not want the world to know. So, don't even get me started.

By the way, despite the thorough cleaning we gave the White House before moving in, we still get this whiff of stinking smell around here. My butler says the stinking smell is from what your dog, Bo, left behind. I disagree. I think the smell is human in origin

– most likely, of a man high on shishi. Another reason why we should not have allowed someone like you anywhere near the White House. You were bad for America. We are going to take care of all the damages you caused.

I am sure that you are monitoring my poll numbers. But just in case you have given up out of frustration, my poll numbers are better than yours at this point in your presidency despite all the stupid norms that I have busted to the annoyance of your establishment type. You will have to deal with having me in the White House for another six and a half years. By the end of which, when anybody says, "Barack Obama," the response will be, "Who?"

That is when I'll know my job is done. It doesn't matter what happens when I am gone. It may interest you to know that I have written my epitaph. It is very simple: "The greatest of all time."

To recap, stay away from my wife, or else…

Yours truly,
Donald J. Trump
The 45th President of the United States of America

Donald Trump's Letter to Mark Cuban

Sunday, April 22, 2018

Hey Mark,

What's up with you? I know you are surprised to receive this letter from me considering our history. But you shouldn't be. Where I am, I have a close-up look at history, and what I see is disgusting. Excuse my French, but history is full of shit. The other day, I spoke with my last divorce lawyer. I might as well reach out to you. There are some things about this place that only billionaires like you will understand.

I know you have mulled the thought of running for president. I want to tell you in all honesty that it is not worth it. Believe me, you have the best life as a private billionaire in America. This office is nothing but a prison. Gene Fowler said, "A fool and his money can go places." But not in the White House. Maybe for poor people like Obama and Clinton who had no plane of their own, it may mean the world. But I can confidently tell you that my life before I came in here was a lot better.

I could do anything I wanted as a private citizen. Now all I deal with are a bunch of people trying to control me. This bullshit place is a prison. Ask Melania. She is having a tough time with menopause, according to Kellyanne. You know that thirty-five years is women's check-out time. I don't know why I'm still married to her at forty-nine. I can't wrap my mind around that number. It is a huge number. It is more like our trade deficit with China.

That you are the strongest man in the world is mere consolation for the prison that you are in. If I am the strongest man in the world, why can't I stop this Mueller witch hunt going on in Washington? Disgraceful. You saw the day Melania slapped my hand down. I could not even put her in her place. Think about it: she couldn't do that when I was not president. Shame.

I am the strongest man in the world, yet reporters like *The New York Times*' Maggie Headshot, or whatever her last name is, are writing rubbish about me, and I am not able to do anything to her. I cannot even get her to sleep in jail for a night. Oh, listen to the greatest bullshit of them all: despite her obnoxious nature, I must still let her into the building where my office is. Can you imagine that? Can you imagine being told that you must allow a stupid sports reporter talking nonsense about you into your Dallas Mavericks arena?

I tell you, I have had it up to here with all these people moving around me, saying, "Sir, sir, sir," yet searching for an adult in the room. What do they mean by that, anyway?

Mark, this is not the game that you and I are used to. There are so many cooks in the kitchen here and so many of them are terrible cooks, especially those Democrats. Believe me, anyone could be president, but not everyone should be. This place is highly overrated.

All around me, there is a sense of history. But the hunt for a place in that book of history is a lot harder than you think. Imagine. I am president, but my pronouncements do not mean much. A Mexican judge could just annul your declaration and executive order in one sentence. What kind of crooked structure is that? At Trump's Organization, I do not need to say a word for things to start happening. Someone like Michael Cohen was trained to read my body language and execute my desires appropriately.

I brought some billionaires in my cabinet hoping that they would be bold and come up with revolutionary changes. But most of them have failed me. If I owned a Dairy Queen, I wouldn't even let them manage it. They make me question how they made their money. Unlike you and I, who worked hard for our money, these people that I have around me obviously inherited their money. Look at that dumb woman that I made Secretary of Education. She doesn't even know her right from left. I would have loved to kick her out and get someone like you who would shake things up and tell me the truth without fear. But somehow, Kelly tells me there have been too many changes of recent and that I should wait for a few more weeks.

Let me make a confession here. Steve Bannon once suggested that I bring you into my administration, but I dismissed the idea. Kellyanne is again suggesting that I should get you into my cabinet a few weeks before the midterm elections. She said it would show the nation that I am grown up, now willing to get a cabinet of equals or something like that. I think that would be huge.

So please write me back and let me know if you would like to join my cabinet. I like your risk-taking persona, and I will give you any cabinet post you want. I think having you out there making things happen will be good for my presidency. And for America too.

I may not have shaved my hair, I may not have trimmed my ego, but goddamit, this place has given me an irritable bowel movement. It is something that I never had before. Disgusting! Very much.

Yours truly,
Donald J. Trump
The 45th President of the United States of America

Donald Trump's Letter to Gen. Michael Flynn

Monday, April 23, 2018

Hi Gen. Flynn,

I hope you are enjoying your laughter. I can assure you, it won't be the last laugh. You bet! This whole bullshit started with you. It was my effort to save your white ass that placed me in this shithole that I am in. If I had known, I would have allowed Comey to roast your behind. I went to bat for you and this is how you pay me back? Very unfair!

No problem. Loyalty, fidelity, courage are all hallmarks of a general. Oh, so much for being a general from the greatest military in the world. Crybaby. So, when you were on the campaign podium with me screaming, "Lock her up, lock her up," you were just a sissy afraid of being locked up. It is very unfortunate. Nasty, nasty character!

A small investigation and you crumbled like a pancake? What kind of man does something like that? What kind of general leaves his troops on the battlefront just to save his behind? Was that how you performed in the military for thirty three years? How do you become an army lieutenant general that way?

You are worse than a deserter. Do you know what the military does to people like you on the battlefield? They get shot in the head. No need for court-martialing. Goddamn it, Flynn! America is a battlefield.

I thought that the first principle to any soldier in any battle is to endure. I thought the second principle is to save your brother-in-arms. I thought that the third principle is not leaving any fallen soldier in the field. I don't get it. Even as you fell, I did not want to leave you in the field. I was preparing to evacuate you, whatever it took.

You were in Operation Urgent Fury, Operation Uphold Democracy, Operation Enduring Freedom, and yet, a small backdoor channel with the Russians was very hard for you to defend. Remember, that was your primary assignment. Nothing more. You were expected to walk up and down that Underground Railroad and wipe away your footprints. That was it. How hard could that be?

You spent a lot of time in the intelligence and counterterrorism areas of the military. Are you saying that you have never encountered situations where you had to take a bullet for the team? I have lost a lot of people who did that for me. I appreciate their sacrifices. I make sure I take care of their families for eternity. If you doubt me, watch how I will take care of Michael Cohen's family.

Even if you didn't want to do it for me, what do you think your cowardice means for the fate of your Flynn Intel Group? Even the Turks won't touch your company with a long pole. Just for $530,000 dollars from the Turks, you flipped sides. From clapping for Turkish exiled cleric Fethullah Gülen and the coup plotters, you quickly switched to the other side, even attending meetings where plans to kidnap Fethullah Gülen were discussed. I wish I knew this about you before. That I even considered you for the position of Vice President was absurd. During the campaign, you were all fired up and saying you were doing everything for the country. Little did I know it was all about you. For a man from the small town of Rhode Island, I expected more loyalty from you.

You were once a good guy. You could be one again. You were damn right about Hillary Clinton's Pizzagate that they now call a conspiracy theory. You did well by pushing it during the campaign at home and abroad. You saved me from being the face of that effective campaign attack. It worked. And I was proud of you. But I cannot say that about your recent moves. Nobody has ever made me contemplate saying for a brief second that Obama was right about anything. But you did. Obama warned me not to hire you as a national security advisor. For that nigga never to think he could tell me what to do and what not to do, I did it.

I do miss your counsel when it comes to issues of Islam. Like I told you, I agree with you that there is no good Muslim as long as Islam remains a political ideology tied to their lifestyle. It is a cancer that must be prevented from further metastasizing, you said. I never forgot that. That was the smart Flynn that I loved. That is why it pains me that you messed up and left me with people who are afraid to defend our position that there is nothing irrational about anyone's fear of Muslims. Nothing.

Because of the choices you made, you have gone from being the national advisor to the greatest president of the United States, to a felon. I bet you will need me to pardon you in the near future. Not looking good at this time!

You lied to Vice President Pence. Big deal! I do that every day. If you had asked me the best way to manipulate Pence into silence, I would have told you. What kind of national security advisor would not carry the president along with him? I know the former Russian ambassador Sergey Kislyak very well. He was helpful when I went to Russia. Very helpful, I must say. No, very, very helpful. If you had told me, he could have corroborated any story you wanted him to. In any case, the Logan Act is an archaic law that I am getting rid of anyway. It is the same with the emolument clause. As soon as I get all these Mueller matters behind me, I will go after all those encumbrances one after the other.

You lied to the FBI. Don't you know there is a limit to where you can be loose with facts? I made time to look at your FBI files recently. I discovered that you have a long history of making up your own facts and believing in them. Your people in the army even called it "Flynn facts." I didn't know that about you when I brought you near me. I am a man who insists on telling the truth. I embrace only verifiable facts, and I like people who work with me to follow the same line – case in point, Kellyanne Conway. How I missed that character flaw in you was a surprise to me.

Greed is not just bad. It is corrosive. That is what happened to you. When you came to me, you should have known that I would make you rich beyond your wildest dreams. Why were you still messing with the Russians and the Turks about money? Ask Michael Cohen. He met me and he had no need to drive taxis anymore. I was going to make you very rich after we were done doing our service to the United States of America. It would have been good. But you did not let it take off. You marred what would have been a great ride from the very beginning.

Even as things stand, if you were loyal to me, I would have protected you still. I always do. If you doubt me, ask my people in New York City. But you panicked because you had no faith.

Your reputation is damaged as it is. And because you are working with that evil man Mueller, I cannot help you. You will spend a long time in purgatory. More importantly, Hope Hicks said that you are fucking up eight generations of your ancestors.

Today is still early. You can still recant. You can still flip back to where you flipped up.

Call Rudy Giuliani if it is something that you are interested in.

Yours truly,
Donald J. Trump
The 45th President of the United States of America

Donald Trump's Letter to Rosie O'Donnell

Thursday, April 26, 2018

Hi Rosie,

You know that I have totally forgotten about you. Very sad! I was just searching for a website where I could buy flowers for Melania to mark her birthday, when I saw your name. Someone at Google should know that the last thing a man wants to see while looking for roses for his wife or girlfriend is your picture. Disgusting image!

How are you doing? Just a few months ago, when I was telling you how inconsequential you were, you did not believe me. See! From where I am, you have never looked so little to me. To imagine that there was a time I was wasting my energy sparing with you on Twitter makes me want to puke. I should have known that you were not worth the time.

As you must see every blessed day, I now dine with the likes of Justin Trudeau of Canada and Emmanuel Macron of France. Terrific guys! With one phone call, I can get any of the 195 presidents of any country in the world to come for dinner in the White House. They love me. Everyone loves me.

How do you spend your days these days? I heard that your most recent girlfriend – is it girlfriend or boyfriend? I don't know anymore and I don't care. I heard that she has dumped your ass and moved on. Who blames her? Who wants to hang around a lousy person like you? Slob! You have gotten two divorces in your bag, just like me, but your fame is waning. Every TV show you get onto, you are fired. Do I need to tell you now that people regret hiring you as soon as you walk into the office? Look at me; I am on the biggest TV show in the world. Kids from Kabul to Kilimanjaro want to be like the Donald. I am the most famous person in the world today. But go to the street of Commack, New York, and ask kids, "Who is Rosie O'Donnell?" They won't have a clue.

I pity those five kids you adopted. I hope you and your cheap nannies don't breed them to be like you. That would be a disaster. What am I saying? With you smoking weed at home, it is absolutely an inevitable end for those poor souls. I am not looking forward to seeing one of them join our military and become decorated like my White House doctor, rear admiral Ronny Jackson. A good man that your liberal type is destroying with unsubstantiated innuendos.

Having reached this pinnacle of life, what I feared most about your kind has been downgraded. I used to fear that gays like you would overwhelm America by breeding your type all over the place. Now I fear those Mexicans and the Muslims. The way they breed all over the suburbs of America is the greatest challenge America faces in the next century. It is not North Korea or Iran. You can see that I am handling those two very well. Things your darling Obama and Hillary could not handle. Weak, weak, weak.

You can be sure that I will solve the Muslim and Mexican problems. John Bolton, that guy is smart, recommended a book to me the other day. He said it is a New York Times bestseller. It is called *Suicide of the West: How the Rebirth of Tribalism, Populism, Nationalism, and Identity Politics Is Destroying American Democracy* by Jonah Goldberg. I told John that I have no time to read books. He summarized it for me. The book says that if I don't do the things I am doing for America at this point, America and the rest of Western Europe will collapse. It made me more resolute in my pursuit.

The Secret Letters of President Donald J. Trump, Age 72

John said that people will mock me and condemn me but that two hundred years from now, I will be held as a hero across the West. An ordained savior, he said. John said my picture will be on the future $1,000 bill. I have already chosen the picture that will be used for the bill. I want it to be a perfect picture of me in my prime, playing golf.

As you can see, I am very busy for your kind. When you see the likes of Bill Maher and all his liberal friends, tell them that I am determined to undo all the regulations and fake climate laws that their darling Obama put in place. Scott Pruitt is doing a tremendous job. There is nothing the lying *New York Times* and *Washington Post* can do about it. If they like, let them bring out a video of Scott killing the last great white rhino left on Earth; he remains my man. Anyone that pisses off the likes of Barbara Streisand and Bette Midler is someone in whom I am well pleased. As for you grumbling about guns, it is now that more sophisticated guns are coming into the market. We will replace apple pie with guns as a symbol of America. If you don't like it, move to Canada.

By the way, I truly thought that some of you would have finished your move to Canada by now. Why are you still hanging around the United States? I don't remember who it was – one of your ultra-liberal kind – that was asked why he had not left. The foolish man said he was waiting to watch my extraordinary fall from power. I think it was Michael Moore; I am not sure.

For those of you Hollywood types waiting, just know that you all are waiting in vain. In no time, I will come around in Air Force One for reelection fundraising in Los Angeles. I am your liberal nightmare, and I am not going away any time soon. So tell your friends to brace up.

Like I told you in the past, what is holding you back are the things you missed when you dropped out of college to become a comedian. It is not too late to return to school and learn a skill. If it is too late for you, at least learn to be nice to people. Bullying people and rudeness block your path to your destiny the same way plaque clogs your arteries. I am sure you understand what I mean. You need to insert the stent of niceness into yourself to make it. If you fail to heed my advice, you may end up the same way your former wife, Rounds, ended. I'm just telling you. I'm just doing you a favor.

Yours truly,
Donald J. Trump
The 45th President of the United States of America

Donald Trump's Letter to His Father, Fred Trump

Thursday, May 2, 2018

Dear Daddy,

Guess what? I am the president of the United States of America. Yep! Your favorite silent film British actor, Frank Dane, was right after all – "Get all the fools on your side and you can be elected to anything."

I know that I never mentioned it as my ambition. But after I had reached the peak of the business world, I needed a new challenge. The only challenge that I found worthy of my genius was to be the president of the United States. And guess what was even more spectacular? I made it in my first try. As you know, over two-third of US presidents tried again and again before they made it. But your big boy made it at first try. I defeated over two-dozen low-energy competitors.

I stunned the world. The whole media of the world, from Cape Town to Casablanca, from London to Las Vegas, screamed that it was unprecedented. The name Trump has gone from adorning the tallest and biggest buildings in New York City to the greatest White House in the world, the official residence of the US president in Washington, DC. If you were still with us, you could just drive into the White House without anybody flagging you down to search your trunk.

You should be very proud, Daddy. Now, whenever your name is mentioned, they have to add "father of the 45th President of the United States of America" Anyone who fails to do that, I can send my FBI to go after them. If I want, I can even sign an executive order saying that anywhere anyone mentions Fred Trump, they must add "Peace be Unto Him" or else… That is how powerful I am.

Remember your first home in Queens? It is now one of the greatest historical buildings in America. In fact, it is considered more important than George Washington's Mount Vernon. My New York City building, Trump Tower, attracts over ten million visitors every year. Imagine that. And I am still the president. When I retire in 2029, I can ask each visitor to pay $100 to look at the building and maybe another $100 to take a picture of the building. You can imagine how much that will bring in a year. Daddy, I can pull in over $1 billion a year just from that alone.

But you know I have my prized possession, my Mar-a-Lago in Florida. That one is already beating Disney World as Florida's destination of choice. People queue to marry in my estate, to have Bat Mitzvahs and numerous conventions. Even some rich amigos are coming to throw sweet sixteen parties for their daughters. I don't care who comes as long as they are paying top dollar.

Daddy, your family is set for the next two hundred generations. From now on, it is winning and winning and winning. As long as the republic exists, nobody will ever mess with the name Trump.

I know you would like to know how I am dealing with the enemies within the deep state. You know those idiots who investigated you for wartime profiteering from military buildings you constructed? Their modern-day evangelists of doom are suing me in court for what they call a violation of the emolument clause for my hotel in Washington, DC. Instead of them thanking me every day for refurbishing the dilapidated Post Office building in DC, they are in court wasting the time of judges that should be handling cases of illegal immigrants. I modified your great saying; "The Trumps are the law wherever they are." When a Trump does something, if it was against the law before, it becomes the law. I told them outright that the law is not meant for a president. Finished!

You know how the US Justice Department in 1973 came after you over how you managed your properties? The same thing is happening again. The way those stupid people wanted to tell you who to let into your own building, saying that you were violating some useless Fair Housing Act and the civil rights of people who had no money to their names – people you extended favors to by allowing them to have a roof over their heads. Well, some people at the Justice Department are foaming at the mouth again. But I will deal with them. And as a Trump, I will put them in their place. You just watch and see.

Some good news—I saved "Merry Christmas." This Muslim man they made president before I came to power to fix things had erased Merry Christmas from our lexicon. He told Americans to say, "Happy Holidays." What a stupid thing to say. Well, I came to America's rescue. I brought Merry Christmas back. In America now, you can once again put up Christmas trees in your living room, and also lights, the way we used to do in Queens long time ago. You are once again allowed to go door-to-door singing Christmas carols. I made it happen. So, tell Angel Gabriel what your son has accomplished. It was a tough war. But as you know, I am a tough guy.

You know, despite your plea that I should follow in the footsteps of my grandfather, I did not go to Karlstadt, Germany, to marry after all. I thank God I went to Slovenia, instead. Our cousins from Germany have not impressed me. There is this one that runs Germany today. She is so stubborn. She won't follow my instructions. And she doesn't look smart no matter how much they say she is. She is the kind of woman that I would have since divorced if I had made the mistake of marrying her.

I know you are worried about my health, as usual. Believe me, I haven't forgotten that Grandpa died in the 1918 flu pandemic. I am very careful about my health. I only eat cheese hamburgers from McDonald's. I'm in very fantastic health. When I was elected president, my doctor said I was the healthiest person ever elected president of the United States. Not an ordinary feat, if you know the line of fat slobs who had held that office. I still wash my hands after any handshake with people who do not look perfect. For instance, I used extra soap after I shook the hands of that sick president of the shithole country in Africa called Nigeria. I still remember your counsel – never take chances with your health.

You know the way you used to tell friends and family that your family was from Sweden, when it was not cool to say that one had anything to do with Germany. I am using alternative facts to escape some tricky situations here. There is this little thing about my lawyer paying some loose woman to keep quiet. I have told them I didn't know about the payment. When it became necessary, I also told them that the money came from the retainer that I paid my lawyer every month. You understand stuff like that. I thank you for preparing me for the kind of things that I encounter here in this godforsaken Washington, DC.

Remember how it took me just three years of joining your company in 1968 to become the president in 1971. In less than two years as the president of the United States of America, I have become the strongest man in the world and the first leader of the free and un-free world. All other presidents before me have only managed to lead the free world. I lead both. For instance, the president of North Korea, that dark and mysterious country that America fought a long time ago, is now my buddy. He calls me when he needs advice. The only problem is that he doesn't understand that we have a time difference. He calls me when I am watching *Fox and Friends*, and that is a no-no.

There was this incident in Charlottesville, Virginia, last year that reminded me of what happened to you in New York City on Memorial Day in 1927, when the Ku Klux Klan marched against assaults by Catholic police. Some native-born people were protesting against the activities of liberals who wanted to remove the statue of our past heroes in Virginia and all over the South. In the encounter, some people were killed. Somehow the liberals wanted me to condemn the natives. They were mad that I said there were some good people on both sides. They don't understand. You were on the KKK side in 1927, and good people like you could be on the other side all the time.

By the way, your friend Benjamin Netanyahu, the former United Nations Ambassador of Israel, is working hand-in-hand with me to solve the other big problem of this world – stopping the rogue nation of Iran from getting a nuclear weapon. He is such a great guy. I am not sure if you know, but Benjamin is the current Prime Minister of Israel. The other day, I sent him to go out there and show the world why we need to destroy Iran and cut them to size.

I must admit, you had an eye for people who had great potential. As you can see, that loan you gave me in 1972 has made all the difference. Like Larry Kudlow said, like an unending stem cell, I have turned it into billions and billions of dollars.

I will keep reporting back to you on the differences I am making in this great nation of ours. But one thing you can be sure of is that I have brought to America the respect that passes all understanding.

I owe it all to your tutelage.

Thank you, Daddy.

Yours truly,
Donald J. Trump
The 45th President of the United States of America

Donald Trump's Letter to Kanye West

Friday, May 3, 2018

Hi Kanye,

Since our meeting in December of 2016, I would have written you before now, but as you know, I have been busy of late. I had to make out time to write the moment I heard that the Pulitzer Prize people gave their prize for music to Kendrick Lamar. What a travesty of genius! It must have been rigged. I'm telling you. Maybe some Mexicans were allowed to vote.

No one deserves that prize more than you. In my world, you have won it again and again. You are the voice of every generation of the last one hundred years and, most likely, the next one hundred years. You deserved it from the first day you came onto the stage with College Dropout. Who else has chronicled the plight of black folks like you? Nobody. Each of your albums is a masterpiece in art.

You see, while Lamar is the Obama of hip-hop, you are the Trump of hip-hop. They will only acknowledge your genius after they have run out of every other option. But people like us who know genius know that you have it. Despite their jealousy and shenanigans, you remain the number one rock star on the planet just as I remain the number one personality on the planet. They cannot take it away from us. Those who have it do not need frontin' (isn't that how all you GED people say it). Those who don't have it, like Obama, go about in Europe fronting.

Like me, you express your genius on and off the stage. You do not strive to be politically correct. You say it the way you see it. That is my kind of man. Not the sissified pussies like Obama who try to please everyone. They shy away from the uncomfortable truth, just to make some weak-minded group feel good about their miserable lives. It has not worked in the last fifty years, and it is not going to work in the next fifty years. Over the years, America has become weak because of people like them.

The future of this country depends on people like you and me. So, I say, be steadfast on your path. It's good that you have a goddess for a wife. My good friend, Howard Stern said that Kim is a piece of ass. Trust me, I believe that. Between you and me, I will join a swing club if you and Kim will join. You know what I mean? Unlike my woman, Kim is comfortable in the limelight. In this business, you need that kind of woman around you. Not the docile sit-at-home ones who know nothing but how to paint their nails and try new clothes and shoes. If I had someone like Kim around me, I would have gotten where I am long before now. I would have made it impossible for someone of Barack Obama's pedigree to be president of the United States of America. (Do you remember his middle name?) That aberration should not have happened in our beloved country. But I am glad that I am quickly wiping away any memory that he was once at the White House.

I'm glad you recognized that Obama did not do any shit for black folks. Of course, like all failures, he has a truckload of excuses. You bravely called out President George W. Bush for not caring about black folks. I think Obama pretended that he cared. He sold a dummy to black Americans that he tried but was held back by Republicans. Now look at what I have accomplished in just one year. The unemployment rate for African Americans is the lowest it has been since recorded history. Any black man who does not have a job now is just too stoned to know where to send his resume. Look at you: you get stoned, but you still perform; you take your psychiatric pills – I heard you take so many? – and you still write great songs. No president in the history of the United States has been able to move black people from the column of poverty to that of prosperity more than I did.

You grew up in Chicago. Just like you, I am concerned about the killing of beautiful young black men on the streets of Chicago. When I am done with this Mueller thing, I will roll out my plan for the inner cities of America. I have Ben Carson working out never before seen strategies – that is, when he is not sleepy. The Democratic plan of constantly taking away guns from black people has failed. In my plan, soon to be announced, I will make it easier for black folks to buy any gun they want. I believe when grandmas in the inner city are known to be packing AR-15s, punks will think twice before they threaten their grandchildren. Just imagine Medea holding an AR-15 or Glock model 19 semi-automatic pistol, 9 mm caliber instead of a tiny handgun. All those street thugs will learn to be polite to grandmas.

Just in case you are wondering, Omarosa told me about Medea. She said it was created by one of your people who is now a billionaire. I told her there could not be an African-American billionaire. She said Oprah is a billionaire. I doubt it. I asked Ben Carson, but he didn't know Medea or her creator. I am not sure if he is trying to burnish his conservative credentials, but he said he never met Oprah.

We need to project you out there beyond one who has accomplished what was once imagined as a fantasy in music, fashion, and business. We need to showcase you as an activist. That is what black folks need more of, your kind of honest true-to-God activism. As you can see, I have restored the fantasy of the white nationalists who were afraid that they had lost their America. I have given them reasons to believe in America again. I think you can be projected the same way, quite the opposite of the hope that the likes of Jesse Jackson, Louis Farrakhan, and Al Sharpton were selling to black people for over four decades now with devastating results.

Obama called his "Audacity of Hope." Since your folks came down from the slave ships, over four hundred years ago, you all have been hooked on hope – hope for a return home, an excursion to heaven, or hitting the lottery jackpot. I think it was your nigga Ice Cube who said that hope and dope are the same. You people have been high on either or both of them at the same time. Muhammad Ali was right to demand manna here on Earth and not wait until you get to heaven to be rewarded.

With a vision of greatness, you started from a basement studio and reached a throne far higher than where the Beatles, Michael Jackson, or even Elvis ever aspired. Twenty-one Grammy Awards are not earned by spending time cutting watermelons and flipping burgers at the barbeque grill, getting high on hope, dope, or both.

By the way, I love the music video of "Bound 2." I can't get Melania to try that with me. She is so boring at times. Sometimes, I envy you. I wish I could rap. It would have attracted lost suburbia white millennials flirting with Nancy Pelosi to my shows. I don't campaign; I put on shows.

My buddy, I love what you said about slavery the other day. That is what I have been trying to tell victimhood-hugging lots like Martin Luther King Jr. Slavery is by choice. We all have the power to choose if we want to be slaves or free people. I'm not a slave to any man or woman. The only person I serve is Donald Trump. I often wonder if I had to teach some of your black folks their own history. Didn't some slaves walk back into the sea at Igbo Landing in St. Simons Island, Georgia, rather than become slaves in America, picking cotton? That is a choice.

You will like this one. I want to work with you to heal the rift between the police and black people across America. You and I agree that the killings of black men by police are at an epidemic level in America, even though I will not acknowledge it in public. Beyond asking black people to obey the police by not running when asked to stop, something has to be done about it. I want you to be the arrowhead in that effort. The way you put Taylor Swift in her place when she stole that MTV Music Award from Beyoncé, that gave you the credibility to lead this effort for black folks. You are tough, and I like that.

While Eric Garner, Michael Brown, Freddie Gray are not really Einsteins in the making, I do not think law enforcement should be killing black men indiscriminately. For good reasons, you should not expect me to blame our police for the killings. That will mess up my PR. And that is where you come in. You can take the shine away from the Black Lives Matter movement and the likes of Jesse Williams by bringing your rational but uncompromising approach to the matter. I will tactically back you up. You have gone through the wire, and I am confident that you will bring that experience to bear.

Kids like Tamir Rice, Laquan McDonald, and Trayvon Martin should not be falling under a barrage of bullets when their age mates in Norway are falling in love on safe and quiet streets. I believe if you champion this, you will overshadow Malcolm X and Martin Luther King Jr. put together. I'm 100 percent sure of this.

I recall you telling me that you used to live in China as a kid. Would you be willing to be my special envoy to China in charge of negotiating intellectual and property rights? Your vision for Tidal has prepared you for such an assignment. If at any time you feel like taking a break from music to do a little diplomacy, just let me know. The job is yours.

All these will help beef up your resume for 2024 when you will run for president to become the truly first black American president – not that phony from Kenya.

Yours truly,
Donald J. Trump
The 45th President of the United States of America

Donald Trump's Letter to His Wife, Melania Trump

Friday, May 4, 2018

Hi Melania,

I will say this just once – stop embarrassing me in public. If you know that you do not want to hold my hand in public, just stay back in the White House. Do not bother to come out. Don't even open the windows or the doors. Turn on the TV and watch classic episodes of *The Jerry Springer Show* while you file your nails. I can get Sarah Sanders to come up with an excuse for you.

If you want sympathy from Americans, I can come up with a story that can make Americans sympathize with you. I can tell Sarah Sanders to announce that you had a miscarriage. You will be adored like Jackie from Camelot, if that is what you want. Only you know that we have not been close to each other in a long time. And try as we can, we cannot deceive Americans on that one. That sucks!

You cannot tell me that it is all these fake stories about what happened in Russia some decades ago that are getting you mad. Or is it that Stormy Daniels's lies? Or is it the Karen McDougal lady? Or it is Summer Zervos? Or is it the crazy Florida woman? Do any of them look like a serious competitor you should worry about? I mean, give me a little credit. Omarosa once told me if I want to eat a toad I should eat a well-endowed one. Do any of them look like a toad that I could eat?

In any case, I am the man. I mean, I know how I rescued you from the slavery of Paris and Milan runways where you were basically selling yourself to the highest bidder. I brought you to this greatest nation on Earth. If you are not dishonest, you should be forever appreciative. It is not as if you were the brightest crayon in the box. What was your IQ again? You dropped out of college after just one year of studying design. And by the way, bimbos like you in Eastern Europe are a dozen a dime.

Tell me, honey, when I met you at Kit Kat Club, what other bright options were there for you? In your family's shithole country of Slovenia, your mother was working in a children's cloth-making company and your dad was a communist selling communist-era cars. What a dazzling future you had ahead of you.

I brought you to the greatest country in the world and gave you a life worthy of princesses like Lady Diana. People like you, from parts of the world you came from, spend a lifetime singing praises of men not worthy of untying my shoes, for just giving then the almighty US green card. Do you know how much women like you pay in dollars and in-kind to get it? Of course, you have zero idea.

I gave you a wedding at Bethesda-by-the-Sea in Palm Beach, Florida, attended by the top two hundred celebrities in America. It was a tremendous *Guinness Book of World Records* event. You wore a $200,000 wedding dress designed by Christian Dior. That is more than the budget of your home country. Not that I expect you to know these things or others of their kind.

Come on, I scooped you off the gutters of Slovenia, and you expect me to tolerate nonsense like frowning your face in public? Let me tell you, don't mess with me. I have billions and billions of dollars at stake in this relationship.

I introduced you to the high society of New York City. You met governors, mayors, Major League players, and great pimps. I'm sure you did not notice that you also met legendary mobsters. I made you the darling of Hollywood. For my grace you were guest in the homes of Hollywood's greatest actors. In Florida, I placed you in a palace better than the Palace of Versailles. What else do you want?

Instead of you waking up each blessed day to worship me, you had the audacity to make faces. You should be kissing every floor my feet touch. Do you know if this was Africa, I would have taken my second and third wives by now? After all, South African Jacob Zuma just married his seventh.

I even brought your parents out of that shithole Slovenia and placed them in a luxury home in the greatest city in the world. I gave them access to the White House. Little woman, what else do you want?

Please, I will say this once. Don't bring out the monster in me. If you like, go and ask my former wives. I'll shake you off at the first sign of any disloyalty. And I don't need to tell you that I have options. After all, now that I am the strongest man in the world, my eyes would not be at beauty queens with their empty heads. I should be looking at princesses of some of the great kingdoms of the world. And all I need to do is point at one and we will have a royal cum presidential wedding at Mar-a-Lago. Wouldn't that be nice?

Whatever you do, remember that you are nothing without me. Don't ever forget that.

Yours truly,
Donald J. Trump
The 45th President of the United States of America

Donald Trump's Letter to Jeff Sessions

Friday, May 4, 2018

Hi Jeff,

What do you think the first line of your obituary will say? "The man whose decision to recuse himself in an investigation being conducted by an agency that he is in charge of led to the destruction of America, which ultimately made America weak again"? Is that what you really want?

I don't want to believe it. You know that you can rewrite this first line so easily. You can turn this narrative around overnight. In just one phone call, you can make it happen. If you do that, we are going to take care of the noble tasks we were elected to accomplish.

I know that you know all these. Why you have refused to choose this noble path in the service of our great country is beyond me. You cannot be tired of winning when we are just starting. What happened to the spirit of the Southern gentleman in you? If anyone had told me that I would have been better off having that Arizonian captured hero cum maverick in my cabinet than you, I would not have believed it.

I have asked Steve Bannon what your problem was. He said that you were protecting the rule of law and zealously guarding your reputation. Big deal! What reputation do you have? You were just an archaic senator from America's shithole of Alabama on your way to the grave when I picked you up from an obvious plunge into oblivion to make you somebody. If I had not done so, you would have died as a borderline racist. I gave you the chance of a lifetime, and this is how you repay me? It sucks so bad!

You know what? Fuck you, Jeff. Fuck out of here. You are a disgrace to the man that you were named after, President Jefferson Davis. You have soiled the nobility of your Confederate roots. I wonder how someone like you, without honor, is allowed to serve in the Army Reserve. Dangerous move, I tell you.

If you think you can bring me down, you do not know where I came from. I am not your sissy Italian mobster who folds up when they hear "Justice Department." Go and ask them in New York City. Go and ask my ancestors in Germany. When we go in, we are all the way in. Nothing scares us. History is full of great Germans who have proved that beyond any reasonable doubt. In your own eyes, I will prove it to you.

I am not Richard Nixon. And you cannot turn me into one. There is German blood flowing in me, not some slimy weak English blood. We are as rugged as the caterpillar. We can withstand heat of up to a thousand degrees. So, fuck you.

If you like, recuse yourself from breathing. Stupid! When I feel it is time to end all this grandstanding, I will step in like a man. With a tweet, I will dump you inside the trashcan of history where you will spend the rest of your life gnashing your teeth. You know I can do it. Totally easy! Or, if I really want to punish you, I will remove Rod Rosenstein, name you a deputy attorney general, and get my ghost personal lawyer, Rudy Giuliani, as the substantive attorney general.

By the way, don't forget those meetings you had with the Russian spook, ambassador Sergey Kislyak. I know some things that you don't think that I know. I know even things about Marion Three that are not yet public. I can force those things that I know down the throat of the dishonest media. You know they love you so much. And trust me, if I want, I can have you spend the rest of your life in prison.

You don't even have the decency to resign your post. So much for Southern charm. You just stand there like an electric pole taking all kinds of embarrassment, dog pee, and flood splashes. I have never seen a man who has no shame like you.

Trust me, you are going straight to hell. I will make sure it happens. Unlike Joe Biden, I will not follow you to the gate. I will have my people bundle you into the bowl of the great American caterpillar and heap you into hell.

…Ungrateful bitch like you.

Yours truly,
Donald J. Trump
The 45th President of the United States of America

Donald Trump's Letter to His Daughter, Ivanka Trump

Friday, May 4, 2018

My beloved Ivanka,

F ine Babe, this is another of Daddy's daily assurances.

I love you.
I love you.
    I love you.
    I love you in ways that pass all understanding.
    Don't mind that Mueller of a guy.
    If he touches you,
    Daddy will start a Third World War.
    I love you.
    I love you.
    I love you.
    I hope you remain amazing for me,
    Always.
    Not for that disposable husband.
    Babe, you are the terrific mirror
    That I'll use

To measure the beauty
Of my next wife.

Yours truly,
Donald J. Trump
The 45th President of the United States of America

Donald Trump's Letter to a Mysterious Woman

Friday, May 4, 2018

Dear Miss Thing,

"Amongst all those who have loved you, I'm the one who has loved you the longest."

"How do you know? What if my first boyfriend still loves me?"
"Not that kind of love."
　"What kind of love?"
　"I'm talking of active love."
　"As opposed to inactive love or passive love?"
　"In active love."
　"What makes love active?"
　"He doesn't go out on a date with you."
　"Do you go out on a date with me?"
　"Sort of!"
　"How? When was the last time you went on a date with me?"
　"Just last week."
　"In your dream?"
　"On your recommendation, we listen to the same music."
　"And that counts for a date?"
　"Yes."
　"I'll ignore that."

"You mean you will check that good for me?"
"Next."
"On your recommendation, we watch the same movies though on different Tvs."
"And that is a date?"
"But we talk about it afterward. That is what lovers do after a movie date."
"What if one of my former boyfriends was watching the same movies too?"
"But not at the same time as we do, and you don't talk about it with him thereafter."
"You are too presumptuous."
"I take that to mean that I've won."
"Whatever."
"I take it to mean that my thesis is valid. Amongst all those who have loved you, I'm the one who has loved you the most."
"You need one more instance to prove it."
"If I give you one more, will you validate it?"
"Yeah."
"Okay. Say he listens to the same '80s music with you, sings it on the phone when you talk, butchering the lyrics. Say he watches the same movies with you. I bet you that he doesn't write poems for you anymore. That is, if he even did before."
"Alright, you win."
"I win?"
"Yeah."
"Please say it twice; let the heavens hear it."
"You are pushing your luck."
"Okay, now that I've won, what are you going to do about it?"
"Longest is not the same thing as passionest."
"There is no word like that – passionest."
"Now that I've said it, there is now a word like that. Yeah. What about passion?"
"You have never given me the chance to show my passion."
"You don't need my permission to let your passion come out. No man does. Passion defies logic."

The Secret Letters of President Donald J. Trump, Age 72

"You moderate passion if only it is weak enough to be moderated. Strong passions are beyond subduing. You know why? Because passion is the stubbornest character we humans have."

"There is no word like stubbornest."

"Again, add it to your dictionary, for now there is."

"But wait, am I hearing you well?"

"It depends on what you heard."

"That dinner lasts longer than sex, but it is sex that is thought about the most."

"Yes."

"Weren't you the one who said I was coming on too strong? Remember? Some twenty-something years ago."

"You know what? I've got a proposal for you. Forget about twenty-one years of seduction. I will see you this weekend."

"Seriously?"

"Yes, seriously. I will fly to Washington, DC, and meet you and break this twenty-one-year-old thirst."

"No way."

"Yes."

"But I have an all-day meeting with the joint chiefs this weekend. Something about a dire situation with Iran."

"Oscar Wilde was right. 'I can resist everything except temptation.' Where should I meet you? Your controversial DC Post Office hotel or mine?"

"Maybe I can reschedule the meeting with the joint chiefs."

"Schiller said that, 'Against stupidity the gods are helpless.' Saturday or Sunday?"

"You know, my chief of staff said—"

"When pleasure interferes with business, our elders warn, give up business. So, what's the best time for you, p.m. or a.m.?"

"And how do I slip out of SSS's sight?"

"My most powerful man in the world, the time is ticking."

Yours truly,
Donald J. Trump
The 45th President of the United States of America

Donald Trump's Letter to Rex Tillerson

Saturday, May 5, 2018

Hi Rex,

You called me a moron. I said nothing. You played your own kettle drum and arrogated to yourself the title, "Adult in the Room." I ignored you. You openly yelled that I was driving on the wrong side of the road. I did not step on the brake. Instead, I accelerated more.

At a traffic stop, I slowed down. I expected you to open the door and jump out. But you didn't.

When you went behind me to poop at my parade ground, I had no option but to send out a tweet that was retweeted by billions of people all over the world.

That is your life, Rex.

That is how you ended your career as the secretary of state of the greatest administration in US history. Total disaster. You had the chance to meet the North Korean leader, shake his hand, and watch the picture published on the front page of every newspaper on the face of this earth. But you screwed up out of greed. Vladimir Putin is ashamed of you. He could still rescind that "Order of Friendship" that he gave you.

Your problem is that you spent a lifetime just digging the ground, extracting what you did not put inside the soil. If you were like me, building mansions out of nothing, you would know how challenging life can be. What else did you do with your life, other than bribe your way through some of the most tyrannical governments in the world? And you call yourself a corporate leader? No wonder you could not manage the State Department that Hillary Clinton turned into her fiefdom.

That was why you could not appreciate the revolution that I am leading. I am working to change the stagnant norms of Washington, DC, that has held our country down. I was obviously expecting too much from a dull and uncreative person like you. I should have known that a man with Hillary-like disappearing emails and a Wayne Tracker alias should not be trusted.

As you go home to write your own book, remember to tell the truth. Do not write the kind of fiction that James Comey wrote. In any case, because you will have me on the cover, you are assured that the book will be a bestseller. Take the money and add it to your retirement account from ExxonMobil.

Have a nice life. I mean it. I will never do the kind of things you did to me. Never! If you are an honorable Eagle Scout and you are honest with yourself, you will have the courage to say that I was the greatest thing that happened to your life.

Ungrateful fool.

Yours truly,
Donald J. Trump
The 45th President of the United States of America

Donald Trump's Letter to John McCain

Monday, May 7, 2018

Dear Senator McCain,

I can see that you are still angry. Even at this dying minute? My friend, get over it. Grow up! Are you going to be bitter till the very end? Isn't there a better way for you to round off your life? Shit! Not that I'm bothered.

But if I were you, I would be making peace with my fellow humans to have a better chance of making heaven. Especially with the kind of life that you lived, you don't need anybody to tell you that the odds of making heaven are against you. But I guess you are so fatalistic that you don't care. What a shame!

Many people said your life went downhill the moment you picked that ignorant woman as your running mate. But I think it started long before that. Long before Vietnam. And it has not stopped even at this late hour. Pathetic! Do take your temper with you as you go, because we don't need it.

I'm giving you straight talk, my friend. Nobody knows about your Manchurian candidacy for president in 2000 better than me. The out-of-wedlock black child might have been fake news, but smart people supported some other stories associated with that.

As a smart guy, I very much agreed with them. You made America look bad when you lost to that African. It was a tremendous stain on America, and the blame be yours for eternity.

Just in case you are wondering, I still have no regret for saying that you were captured and that I like my heroes to be those that avoided capture. It is a hard call, but someone had to make it. If one is captured, for him to be a hero, he has to break out of captivity. That is what James Bond does. But sitting in prison for eternity waiting for negotiations and trade-offs and trade-ins is not a mark of a hero in my eyes. That is why courage matters. No apologies for that.

It is funny that we could have gotten along quite well, being that you love beautiful women too and have married more than once. You also share with me that slippery dance that happens when you transition from one marriage to another. It is just that your hothead would never let you see how amazing I am.

For antagonizing me since I came to shake up Washington, DC, and for voting to keep that dreadful Obamacare alive, I say to you what Anthony Scaramucci taught me: *Cagati in mano e prendit a schiaffi* (meaning, "shit in your hand then slap yourself in the face.")

Let me make one thing clear to you. I am not into going to funerals to begin with. So you are wrong – the right to show up at your funeral is not worth fighting for. When a motherfucker is dead, I let the dead bury their dead. How do I say this in a politically correct way – I consider some deaths nature's way of helping me to drain the swamp. So don't think I will miss a thing because I won't be at your funeral.

If you invite me to a wedding, I will be there. I love weddings. That is why I feel bad that Prince Harry did not invite me to his wedding. I heard that it was all because of Obama politics taken too far. Anyway, English food is horrible to begin with.

As for your funeral, you can have vice president Mike Pence. Frankly, isn't attending funerals of less important people why we have vice presidents? That is the tradition. Excuse me. It is not as if you would know. You haven't smelt the presidency.

When important people die, like queens, kings, and presidents, I will be there.

So, amigo, don't waste the few remaining sleepless nights on me.

Yours truly,
Donald J. Trump
The 45th President of the United States of America

Donald Trump's Letter to President Emmanuel Macron of France

Thursday, May 10, 2018

Bonjour President Macron,

I did it! Yeah, very easy. Did you watch? Did you see how I was hailed from Iowa to Israel for doing it? Nice people. They are on with the program.

Did you see how stupid your fears were? Did I not tell you not to be a crybaby about it?

Forget about those ignorant people's dance of death in Tehran. We have seen it before. They should know by now that rather than fear death, America takes selfies with death and moves on. What is more stupid than buying American flags and setting them on fire? The more they burn, the more flags we make for them to buy and burn. I just hope those flags they were burning were not made in China. Believe me, that is the reason for my textile tariff.

You thought if I announced America's withdrawal from the unfair and terribly bad Iran nuclear deal that Tehran would bust into a fireball that would engulf the old and new walls of Jerusalem? I told you that you sounded unbelievable. See how right I was?

Your problem, like I said during that magnificent, never been seen state dinner at the White House was that you were listening too much to those two old and childless women of Europe. Don't say that I did not warn you. They can be very nasty. I know women like those. They are always hysterical over nothing.

I told you that I am an expert on women affairs. Trust me, women make things bigger than they actually are. That is why I like to have them always subdued, if necessary, barely able to speak English. Those women are easier to handle. This type that you have, all around you in Europe, want to be on top of the man. I don't let that happen. We can't let that happen.

For extremely stupid people in your country who would scream that the sky is falling, just let them know that all I did was correct Obama's reckless mistake. Those who said that I fired the first shot of the Third World War, please tell them to stop being ridiculous. You can guarantee them that the only thing that would make me contemplate something as drastic as starting a Third World War is any attempt by Mueller to attack my beloved Ivanka.

You saw her when you visited. You agreed with me that she is extremely beautiful. She is the only person worth putting my country on the line for. As for me, I am the president, and I am the law. Nothing the president did, does, or will do is against the law. It is in the Constitution. If they don't like it, so bad. Let them go and be president.

Now, about what happens next. I know that this is one thing troubling your Europe wannabe Amazon ladies. Just tell them that Bibi and I have them covered. At our time of choosing, we will announce that Iran is restarting its nuclear weapon program. Once Bibi announces it, I will tell my CIA boys to second Bibi.

Then the war starts. At every opportunity that Bibi and I have, we will bomb Iran's nuclear weapon facilities. It will be spectacular. Like Syrian attacks, only one thousand times more brilliant. My generals told me we can overwhelm Tehran with fire and fury until everyone in that country is on their knees begging me for mercy. It is the kind of language that they understand.

The Saudis are thrilled. As a thank you, they are spending some billions of dollars for our fighter jets. These are jets that you and I know are out of fashion. And I doubt if they have pilots that can make them roar in the night sky the way the American pilots they were built for fly them and can make them blaze. You know fighter jets are like women: in the wrong hands they just lie there on the bed, dormant and cold. But in the right hands, they are fired up, hopping up and down the sky like antelopes. Have you seen antelopes making love before?

My Jews are happy about what I plan to do in Iran. It means that my reelection campaign coffers will be buoyant in a few weeks. If Michael Cohen had not screwed up, his LLC would have been getting millions in deposits per hour. There would have been no need to depend on Putin's friends to funnel money to me through Michael.

Just for your information, this is very confidential. Don't even let Brigitte, your teacher wife, hear about this. My bottom line is that I need insurance against impeachment from all of Mueller's shenanigans. The Koreans were trying to be smart asses. They were scared of their countries being used as a theater of war, so they pulled together. The Shia in the Middle East are eternal mortal enemies, so nothing can change that. A president that is at war is a president that has perpetual immunity from everything. He cannot be impeached or even be criticized while the nation is at war. Never happens.

Forget Nixon. That one was a crook. I, Donald J. Trump, I'm not a crook.

About sanctions. I am re-imposing sanctions against Iran. What it means is that any European company caught doing business with Iran will be barred from doing business with the United States. It is that simple. You are either with us, or you are against us. No exceptions. If you need to translate that into French for your old hens of Europe, please do.

John Bolton said that I am the twenty-first century Winston Churchill. He said in our own eyes I am quickly transforming into the man Churchill, with this simple decision on Iran. Once again, I would be the one who saved the West. You have an opportunity to be my Charles de Gaulle. So, I offer you this deal. You will be my Charles de Gaulle. Putin will be my Roosevelt. And I will be Winston Churchill. Together we will remake the world in our own image.

You just need to stick with me and not with those appeasers of Chamberlain-type that I see in Merkel and May. Get on my strong wings and let us ride into the starlight.

This is the only thing that I ask of you. When I am done with Iran and with flushing Muslims out of Europe, because that is coming next, I will want the Eiffel Tower renamed after me. You tell that woman in London to rename Trafalgar Square or Heathrow Airport after me. Anything short of that would be a sign of ungratefulness. As for the Germans, anything short of renaming their capital city after me would be unacceptable. After all, I am their grandson who found success in America. Wouldn't it be great to rename London Trump?

To celebrate Europe's liberation, you should all throw a party for me. Since Europeans don't work on Wednesday, I want a parade from Elyse Palace across the English Channel and ending at Trafalgar Square. I will be in an open-top limousine waving along. You can stand beside me. If you need a befitting woman by your side, I can get you one of the world's best. I own Miss Universe, you know.

The other day, some smart people were so impressed by my strategy in Iran that they offered me a book deal. It's happening already. They want me to write how I arrived at this marvelous decision on Iran and maybe sprinkle other stunning decisions of my young administration. I scribbled a proposal down for them. I tentatively called the book, *The Secrets of President Donald Trump's Genius* or *The Secret Letters of President Trump*, or *Inside President Donald J. Trump's Head*. They were over the roof with excitement about the best-selling prospects of the book. But I don't want to benefit from the services that I am selflessly rendering to America.

As a result, I decided to have the book published under a pseudo name: John Barron, John Miller, Rudolf de Passe, or

David Dennison. You know, one of those names that I use when I speak anonymously to the media or when I need to sign something discreetly. Some of my people prefer Rudolf Hess because it would resonate with my German heritage. The final choice of name and title are of course left for the publisher to choose.

I showed the outline of the book to some book reviewers, writers and friends in the publishing industry, and these are the reviews that I got.

Praises for *The Secrets of President Donald Trump's Genius*.

"Rudolf Hess should be arrested and locked up for breaking into president Donald Trump's brain. How he came out alive is something that I'm sure the Russians are investigating."
—*New York Daily Apple*

"Don't pick this book up unless you are willing to let reason, your reason, crumble as soon as laughter tickles it."
—*Miami Bell*

"Rudolf Hess must have been dropped on a hard floor when he was a toddler. There is no other way to explain his unique madness."
—*Washington Ghostwriters*

"You must not read this fucking book if you do not want to be offended. LOL. I'm not kidding."
—*London Daily Chips*

"If you do not find yourself screaming at some of these letters, then you are a conscientious objector carried away by your chuckles."
—*Publishers' Slush Pile*

"For making me spill my coffee on my pants, sorry, groin, I say fuck eight generations of your ancestors."
—*Moscow Golden Shower Times*

"Be ready for your conscience to lose its virginity before you open this book. You will not come out the same way you went in, even if you are president Donald Trump."
—*European Rags of Paris*

"Rudolf Hess has sprinkled lies into non-fiction the same way Bill Cosby sprinkled drugs into women's drink, with the same effect."
—*Philadelphia Evening Answers*

"This Trump is smarter than the one in the White House." Grace Upbeat, the author of *My Nuclear Button Is Bigger than Yours*.

"For spending this much time inside Trump's head, I hope Rudolf t.g. Hess is forced to pay rent." – Tony Bacharach, DC Attorney.

"I don't care who you are, this Trump will surprise you in some pleasant ways as you read these letters. Sometimes, against his best interest, he is really really pee your pant funny." - Jasper Bush, Rock Musician.

"Finally, I understood Donald Trump's mind. Thank you, Mr. Hess." – Michael York, Homeless New Yorker.

So, my friend, don't panic. Hang around, and everything will be alright.

Yours truly,
Donald J. Trump
The 45th President of the United States of America

Donald Trump's Letter to Oprah Winfrey

Saturday, May 12, 2018

Dear Oprah,

Congratulations on your speech at the Golden Globe Awards. That was great. Now say, "Not again."
Repeat.
One more time.
That is how I will end your 2020 presidential campaign. I will remind Americans not to make the same mistake for a second time. They allowed themselves to be mesmerized by Barack Obama, the 2000 Democratic Party one-speech wonder, resulting in unmitigated disaster.
Luckily for America, I came around to mitigate the disaster Obama brought on this great nation.
My generation, the greatest generation, did not allow Jesse Jackson to fool them with speeches full of fluff signifying nothing. But this good-for-selfie generation fell for Obama's empty talk from an empty barrel.
Not anymore. So, shove your Golden Globe speech and return to your TV talk show.
Otherwise, if the Democrats are stupid enough to nominate you for president, I will start writing my second inaugural address.

I will beat you so silly that your brand will never survive. If you are their nominee, Melania will start writing her convention speech on time so that she won't plagiarize someone else's speech.

You will recall that as far back as 1999 when I started thinking of running for president to rescue America and make our country great again, I have flirted with the idea of picking you as my vice president. I thought that as someone born in poverty to a single mother in the deep Southern state of Mississippi, that your story of overcoming tremendous obstacles to become one of the richest people on Earth would inspire many disillusioned Americans. I have not given up on that idea.

You are still a terrific woman. Great in the things you do. But politics is not one of your strengths. You are not good at it. And most women that I know are not good at it either. You women are too insecure and too emotional to succeed in politics. Don't look at Theresa May in the UK and Angela Merkel in Germany. Those individuals are not women. They are almost men. And to make matters worse, in those countries, men are no longer men. I don't need to sugarcoat this. European men have reached the end of their feminization. And that disease is what I'm trying to prevent in America with the disinfectant that I'm spreading after the dung that Obama left behind.

Before this noise about you running for president, I had a secret team that I commissioned to work on how to drop Mike Pence as my vice president in 2020 and pick you as his replacement. I felt your inclusion on my team would help heal America. At first, it would break the hearts of American liberals. But the moment they realized that I was handing over to them on a platter of gold the presidency of the United States, they would embrace the idea—and proclaim my genius.

I still want to believe that you were just teasing them on this quest to be president.

In some ways, you remind me of myself. You took a third-rated talk show out of Chicago and made it an international hit of a TV show. It is the same thing that I did with my father's Queens Village company. I took it to number one real estate company in America.

Through your show, you gave an opportunity for the underrepresented to become part of the mainstream. That is exactly what I did with the Trump Organization. All those Mexicans who would otherwise not find jobs in America because they did not speak English or had no education, I gave them jobs and paid them enough to feed their families and have more to send to their relations in Mexico. One day, I will get the accolades that I deserve.

You, however, did something impressive for which I want to bring you closer to me. After swimming in the gutters with the likes of Jerry Springer, Jenny Jones, Ricki Lake, and Phil Donahue, you made a sharp U-turn. You raised the level of talks that you engaged in on your show. You embraced self-help and pseudo-spirituality. It soon transformed you into a guru. That is exactly the kind of transformation that I want in my second term in office.

I want to elevate the discussion and the language. I want the world to know that I am not an idiot. For crying out loud, I went to an Ivy League university. I cannot do it alone. I need someone around me that I respect to be a partner in that healing process. All the people around me now are the "Yes, sir" types. They don't have confidence in their own thoughts. When I push back just a little, they fold up.

It is hard to believe now that you once won the Miss Black Tennessee beauty pageant. Such an accomplishment matters a lot to me. Probably the same way that black life matters to you. I'm sure if you had lived in a decent part of America that my eyes would have caught you long before you became a national figure. Who knows, I would have taken you by my wings and got you to rise to the top faster than it took you. It is exactly what I did for Melania and so many other women, most of whom would not acknowledge it.

How is Steadman doing? I guess that 1992 marriage ceremony is not going to happen after all. I feel it was a right move on your part. You don't need a partner around you who is feeling entitled. It is better to leave the buffoon hanging around without a designated title or legally binding tag. That way the public will lower their expectations of you. If you don't feel like holding hands in public, you don't have a sense of obligation that you should do it because others are doing it. You know what I'm saying?

You know I did not need your Oprah Effect to get my book as the number one best-selling book of the twentieth and twenty-first century, so even if you decline this offer, I will still accomplish all that I set out to accomplish. Though I am on course to reverse all that Obama did at the White House, I have no intention of rescinding the Presidential Medal of Freedom that Obama gave you in 2013. I would have given that to you if Obama did not do so. And if I had given it to you, it would have been more prestigious and more praiseworthy instead of being seen as mere act of nepotism from Obama.

I still love you, Oprah. Despite your touchy-feely style, you are a fantastic woman. When I am done fooling all these poor folks in rural America with their dogs, smell of gunpowder, and dream of manna from heaven, I will rejoin the elite.

Remember December 1, 2005, when you appeared on *The Late Show* with David Letterman, thereby ending your eleven-year feud; I want to invite you to the White House as my reelection campaign approaches. I want you to be the moderator as I host former presidents, all of whom are not talking to me now. It would be like the eightieth birthday party you threw for Maya Angelou at my wonderful Mar-a-Lago club. I could use that opportunity to announce you as my running mate. What do you think? Believe me, it would shake up Washington, DC. Oh, by the way, come with Gayle. Nice lady!

To be quite frank with you, I hope this doesn't count as Oprahfication. I believe you are like me deep down – a hustler with a great sense of timing. There must be something we can do together – you and me. Unlike Obama, I don't need an endorsement from you and the one million primary votes you gave Obama. I fly with my wings. Instead, what I need from you is to have you as my running mate as I predicted in 1999.

Spend a little time and think about this. This is how history will record our partnership. Oprah was the woman who came and tamed Donald Trump. Let the dishonest media celebrate that I have accepted the gospel according to Oprah. I don't give a hoot. After Donald Trump, then comes Oprah, the first female president of the United States of America. That would be the icing on the cake of your great achievements.

Yours truly,
Donald J. Trump
The 45th President of the United States of America

President Donald Trump's Secret Letter to Prince Harry

Thursday, May 24, 2018

Dear Prince Harry,

Congratulations on your wedding. I watched a little bit of it. I wish I could say that it was terrific. But I can't. In fact, it was horrendous. Believe me, it was too painful to watch. I'm sure the ratings were in the gutters.

What was that cheap thing that your bride was wearing in the name of a wedding gown? Awful! I know that your father is unemployed, but if your grandparents had fallen on hard times, you should have reached out to me for help. I could have asked some shell companies to wire some money to your shell account. It was such a disgrace of a wedding gown. For crying out loud, you are a prince. Or are you not? I now regret more that I did not get the chance to date your mother. I would have had the chance to impart on you a little bit of my marvelous taste in style and women.

Didn't you and Meghan take a look at what my Melania was wearing during my wedding? That picture is beautiful people's first stop for inspiration as they plan for their wedding. *All Styles Magazine* called it the "gold standard." And what is up with

Meghan not putting on makeup? The cake may be sweet on its own, but it still needs the icing. You see, I pleaded with you to consult me, but out of fear of your grandparents, who were playing fake diplomatic politics, you didn't. You missed a wonderful opportunity to make Britain great again. You messed up bigly.

Oh, where did you dig up Rev. Jeremiah Wright? I thought Obama kept him in a witness protection program? I'm talking of that pastor that preached at your wedding. Disgusting! How could you subject your grandparents to that torture? You make America look bad. If you had told me that you needed an American preacher, I would have given you one of our very fine preachers, like Pastor John Hagee. He is a great guy. He would have spoken in good English that your grandparents would have understood, and not Ebonics.

And that nasty black woman conductor for the "Stand by Me" singers… how did she get into that church? Through which door? She was not good for your reputation. It totally sucked. You know what? I will give you and Meghan a great deal. Come over to Mar-a-Lago for your honeymoon, and I will help you repair the damage your whole wedding debacle did to your reputation. Don't worry about the dishonest media. I will keep them off my property for the period that you are there.

I have a lot of things to discuss with you, including how to handle the upcoming election for the next King of England. I have some friends who could help you beat the establishment candidates. In the meantime, I have to run. I will write you at another time. General Kelly has this North Korean thing that he wants me to look at.

Yours truly,
President Donald J. Trump
The 45th President of the United States of America

Donald Trump's Letter to Kim Jong-un

Sunday, May 27, 2018

Dear Chairman Kim,

I write to ask you to ignore the public letter I just sent you. I was just trying to distract the dishonest media. Lucky you, you don't have to deal with such irritation. The first task of your media is to dress you up in your Sunday best. Anyone who goes out of line goes out of circulation. That is how presidents should be treated all over the world. Damn it, I admire the respect that you are accorded by your countrymen. I bet no late-night comic makes fun of you at night. These are some of the indignations that I have to deal with. Totally unacceptable.

The second reason I canceled the meeting was to reestablish that I am the boss. Everything happens because I want it to happen. There is no other way things happen in the era of Donald Trump. Some retarded people are beginning to suggest that you and I should share the Nobel Prize with the low-energy South Korean leader and the cunny poker-faced chairman Xi Jinping of China. I don't think so. Now that you and I have done the heavy lifting, taken all the risks, they are loitering around to take part in the glory. I won't let them.

The third reason I canceled the meeting was to give the Russians time to take care of something for me. In this chess game that we play, time makes all the difference.

The fourth reason I canceled the summit was because of my vice president. He was hurt by the name your people called him. I had promised him that I would do something about the name-calling shit. My canceling of the meeting was my way of making him happy. He is a sensitive man, but my bitch still. His Christianity is phony though, but nobody is ready to tell him that. He clings to prayers the way some old bitches cling to phony tits to get ahead.

Despite what the fake news media is blabbing, I am sending my people to come and meet your people. Not only are we still looking forward to Singapore, but also we still hope to have it take place on June 12. I have checked every other day in June and July in a history book. The twelfth is the only day that nothing important has happened in history. I want the day of our meeting not to share historical pages with any other event.

After my people meet your people at the DMZ, you can send your best man to New York City for a meeting. Your man will definitely be given America's unbeatable hospitality. Whatever he wants in New York City, we shall make it available to him. If he wants to stay at the Trump Tower, we will make the penthouse available to him. What is important is that we hold this historic summit and stun the world of doubters.

I'm sure you understand my strategy.

Yours truly,
Donald J. Trump
The 45th President of the United States of America

Donald Trump's Letter to a Kid Separated from Parents at the US Border

Tuesday, June 19, 2018

Hello lil' amigo,

Once upon a time, there was a little mermaid lost on the Pacific Sea, trying to make its way to the Atlantic. She has one lifeline left—popping onto the great American ship named Donald Trump.

Forget it! Why am I wasting time with a folktale? It is not as if you have the cognitive skills needed to understand what I am saying.

Let me cut to the chase. How are you? I hope you are enjoying the United States. Isn't this the greatest country that you have ever seen? I'm sure it is. You must have been enjoying our wonderful meals—hamburgers and hot dogs. I bet you have never tasted anything like those. Did you eat our watermelon? I heard you people like that.

I'm fully aware of the sad condition of the shithole country where you were born. It is unfortunate. But it is not my own making. By that I mean, it is not America's making. It is a matter that you need to discuss with your God when you see him. He chose to put you there. Ask him why.

A friend of mine here at the White House, who believes in Eastern religion, says that your lot in life is a result of what you did in your last life. If he is right, it means that you were naughty in your last life. As a result, you were condemned to be born in Guatemala, El Salvador, or Honduras. In your last life, you were probably a rapist or you were bringing drugs into the United States. It has to be one of those. Just accept your punishment.

If you live a better life this time, maybe in your next life, you will be born in the United States. That way, you don't need to sneak into our country with your mother – that is, if she is really your actual mother. Believe me, we know there is nothing you guys will not do to get into God's own country—the United States.

I am building the wall to keep little pricks like you out. It looks harsh right now, but at the end, it will be good for you. You pay your dues, your debt to your society, and in your next life, you will have a better life. But if I allow you to sneak in here, claiming political asylum, you miss an opportunity to repent. Without repentance, your sin will follow you along.

Another way to look at it is that if you all leave your damned countries, who is going to fix them? The United States of America is not interested in nation building abroad. We want to build up our own nation first. Do you catch my drift?

Come to think of it, your parents complain that they were running away because of gang violence and all that. I laugh in German when I hear that. What kind of violence is in Guatemala, Honduras, or El Salvador? Is it anything compared to what we have in Chicago where Obama's thugs are openly and happily destroying the city? Do you see kids and their mothers leaving Chicago for Mexico, Cuba, or the Dominican Republic? No. Chicago parents and their kids are not even packing up to climb into a Greyhound bus for a few hours' trip to Canada, Iowa, or Madison. They are not buying the Eldorado tales about life in Canada, Iowa, or Madison. They are staying put to fight for their hometown. That is what I expect your folks to do.

For those mothers who say that domestic violence is the reason they are running away, have they bothered to look at the statistics about domestic violence in America? There are twelve million victims of domestic violence in the United States every year. That is more than three percent of the US population. In the White House here, the percentage is even more.

Imagine if those twelve million men and women with their kids headed south of our border. Where would they settle? Mexico would not contain them. Who would provide for them? Are there cages in Haiti for Americans running away from domestic violence? Would the UN nonsense asylum expectations cater to the twelve million Americans each year?

I heard that your parents are telling you that the man stopping you from enjoying a good life in America is the Nebuchadnezzar of our time. I know Jeff Sessions. He is not a Nebuchadnezzar. He is a glorified sissy. He does not have what it takes to be a great king like Nebuchadnezzar. So when you hear that fairy tale, don't pay any mind to it.

I'm sure some of you have listened to those talking heads on TV who compare your living situation to cages. You and I know that it is 100 percent better than where you came from. That you enjoy running water and modern toilet facilities in the housing we provided you is something to be appreciative of. Some Americans in Alabama do not have such amenities. Even in New York City housing authority buildings, water tanks have Legionnaires' disease while tenants endure winter without heat in their homes. So be thankful. Don't think for a moment that we don't know that you came from where you drink untreated well water and water from polluted streams and that you defecate inside the bushes or in pit latrines. We know, amigo. We know.

So I advise you to just tell your parents to calm down. Let them enjoy it while it lasts because we are determined to send you back to where you came from. For you, consider this visit as a camp, summer camp in America. When you get back home tell those still planning to make the trip that America is closed.

Yours truly,
Donald J. Trump
The 45th President of the United States of America

Donald Trump's Letter to Roseanne Barr

Sunday, July 1, 2018

Dear Roseanne,

I'm sorry to read that the liberals who run television networks in America have gotten rid of you. I can talk to my people at Fox television to get you a spot at that brilliant network. My only concern is that you often operate like a lone ranger. You are incapable of taking instructions from anybody. There has to be someone out there that you listen to. You cannot operate on your own whims. Who do you think you are? Donald Trump?

See, let me tell you a secret. You can do anything you want to black men. But black women are a protected species. Before you attack them, you have to make sure they are damaged goods like Maxine Walters. Trust me, just like you, I didn't know that bitch was black. I thought she was Arab. That was what scared me the most about her. That she might, just like that Crooked Hillary's Arab assistant, be sending information to Israel's enemies. You never can tell with those people.

If I were to compare her to an animal, I would not have gone for an ape. I would have said a ram. You know, those stinking, angry-looking animals with oversized balls. But, yeah, I'm a nice guy, so I will leave it at that.

People in Washington do not understand my genius. It may look as if I attack people indiscriminately. But, no, I don't. Believe me, there are hours of calculations put into any tweet that I send out. Even the typographical errors are planned in advance. As for the grammatical errors, they are put in there to obstruct and distract the little-minded ones who do not see the big picture.

What baffled me was your reaction to being fired. Why did you beg those knuckleheads at ABC not to cancel your show? It made you look weak. People who voted for me do not fold like that. They attack. When they go high, we drag them down. When they go low, we get a shovel and dig up dirt all around them until they sink deeper.

Why did you blame Ambien for the tweet you sent? I like Ambien. I get it all the time on Air Force One when I am going to important meetings abroad. Let me tell you, once they see that you sound weak, they bounce and pounce even more. Instead of reasoning with them, reminding them that the advertisers were not bailing out and that you were ready to go on TV and explain yourself, you should have been threatening to send a truckload of lawyers to sue them into oblivion.

If you had called me before speaking with them, I would have told you to wear your Hitler mustache and swastika armband, grab your crotch, and spit at them once again. The joke is not on you. It is on them. But if you really wanted to explain, you should have told them that the stress of being the number one show on American TV reactivated the traumatic injury you had when you were a kid, following that accident. You could have said that the numerous psychiatric drugs your doctor prescribed for you were making you lose touch with reality. Liberals love to sympathize with people like that.

When I called you to celebrate the success of your reboot show, I told you I could connect you to a great talent agency far better than ICM. You may have to do a deeper tummy tuck, tighter breast reduction, wider gastric bypass, and a precision nose job to fit in. But I'm not worried. You are used to those adjustments that come with being a major TV star. There is nothing anyone can do about your ugly face. But those who say you are unattractive are not seeing your inside. Once I am done with this presidency thing, I'm signing up with the agency, and that is when I will become much more than the greatest star in the world.

Did I just hear that ABC is moving ahead without you? How could you allow them to do that? It is your show, after all. When I left NBC, on my own terms, I only allowed them to carry on with *The Apprentice* because even though I wasn't there, I was still getting paid for every episode they made. That is smart thinking on my part. As it showed, the failures of the shows made after I left proved that I was the main attraction of the show. That big mouth of a failed actor, Arnold Schwarzenegger, was a total disaster. What is he doing with his life now besides being the babysitter of the amigo child he had with his house cleaner?

Do you still take marijuana for glaucoma? I don't want you to despair. Junior is working on starting a TV network, Donald Trump Network, DTN. If you keep your brain sharp, we can get you a spot on the network. Mind you, it won't be the tear-jerking kind of thing that Oprah is doing at OWN. In the meantime, let John Goodman and co. keep fooling themselves thinking that they are making a spin-off. Their fate will be the same as the fate of all those Republicans who think they can win elections without me. They have started to see that they are nothing without me. Democrats will devour them without my muscles. That is the same with you.

Until then, keep spending the money you have already made. And prepare to run for political office again in 2020, though I advise you not to go straight to a run for president. Winning the presidency in the first try without any political experience happens once in a century. It takes a special legend to accomplish that. I'm not saying this because I did it. It is just the plain truth.

Yours truly,
Donald J. Trump
The 45th President of the United States of America.

Donald Trump's Letter to Queen Elizabeth

Sunday, July 15, 2018

Dear Queen Elizabeth,

I thank you for your warm welcome when Melania and I visited Windsor Castle. We appreciate all the efforts your majesty government made to make sure we were comfortable.

Despite not curtsying to you, which was a minor oversight, I have no doubt that we greatly impressed you. You only got a glimpse of why I loom larger than life wherever I go. It is a humongous gift that I have. Unbelievable! Isn't it?

I understand that I was the twelfth US president you have hosted. I don't need to be told, but I know you consider me one of a kind. You are not alone. I dazzle people everywhere I go. I remind them of a long-gone era when men were men and politicians were what the people wanted them to be.

Before I came, I took a crash course in your country. I was quite impressed by the things I learned. I had thought before then that you all were women, just sissies, with the exception of Winston Churchill. I was surprised that you joined the Second World War and were trained as a mechanic.

If another Vietnam War were to start, you bet I would be first to go to the war front. I missed the last one because I had bad feet. It has since been resolved when I stood on my own.

Did Churchill really say that at age two you had an air of authority and reflectiveness astonishing in an infant? Did he? It is historic that you have met five popes. You are now the longest-lived, longest-reigning British Monarch, but that is not enough. To what end? That is the question. In less than two years, I have accomplished more than Obama could do in eight years.

Since I am the last US president that you will ever meet, I think you should consider renaming one big institution in London after me. Stick it to the face of those ignorant protesters wasting their miserable lives on the streets of London while I was with you in Windsor. Do it as a reminder to that sleeper cell Muslim punk in London city hall, of who truly owns the land. Trust me, it would be the most lasting legacy of your sixty years on the throne. I can reciprocate by renaming the old lady of the White House, the West Wing, the Queen Elizabeth Wing. I know you will like that.

As a smart leader and former host of *The Apprentice* I have assessed your son Charles. I don't think he has the backbone needed to return the failing United Kingdom to its coveted place in the world. He looks weak, like a man that Camilla orders around. Without telling you how to run the affairs of your Kingdom, I think you should state in your will that the crown should skip Charles and go to Prince William. That is the only hope the monarchy has to rejuvenate itself after you. Charles will do to the United Kingdom what Obama did to the United States—turn it into a feminine nation of welfare-dependent bleeding-heart liberals.

I don't need to warn you about that Obama-lit American that Harry brought into your distinguished family. Bad choice! She may look harmless but going by the damage that Obama brought on the United States, I can tell you that she has the potential of ruining the great tradition of your noble family. I know she and her generation will never come near the line of succession, but they can pollute the Windsor family tree. Before they scream "racist," you and I know that I am not a racist, but I personally think it is contaminated as it is. If Harry had told me that he wanted an American woman, there are a lot of fine, smart, and clean

American girls I could have hooked him up with. Not that eh… what again did Omarosa say Peter Tosh called such girls? Yeah, "brand-new second-hand girls." He could well have married Stormy Daniels.

That was one reason why I did not date your late daughter-in-law, Diana. I fancied her a lot, at one point. I even made moves. I sent some bouquet of the finest flowers money could buy. But as I found out now, she had this thing that most of your subjects have about gum-chewing ugly Americans. Since your uncle, Edward VIII's abdication, after marrying divorced American socialite Wallis Simpson, your people have looked at our people with suspicion. It shouldn't be so. We may be cowboys, but we have our hearts in the right place.

How could you even feel that way about us, the beautiful Americans? Your husband's sister married a Nazi. And your husband was foreign-born, from Europe's shithole country of Greece. He wasn't even Anglican. So, what are we saying here?

Since my visit, a thought has remained with me. As far back as 1929, you were born by cesarean section. Great feat, then. So, whatever happened to the Great Britain that I read about in the history books? Your kingdom is losing so badly in ways that matter. Did all your smart and courageous men and women leave for the United States? An extremely credible source told me that you failed to build a great wall, allowing the Irish to flood your country and neutralize your strength. Seriously, how was it that you were left with men with crooked teeth and weak spines, like Theresa May? Oh, I forgot, he is a woman. Lol.

Now let me say the most amazing thing you ever heard. I hope you remember it for the rest of your life. I find you very hot, grandma. It was a surprise to me. I hope you don't take any offense. Consciously or unconsciously, I did not expect that. I'm just being me. At one point I was afraid of being left alone with you in the palace. Just saying. Imagine the president of the United States hooking up with the Queen of England in Buckingham Palace or in a Treetop Hotel in a jungle somewhere. Now that would be the greatest movie of all time.

I hope it makes you smile whenever you remember it.

Yours truly,
Donald J. Trump
The 45th President of the United States of America

Donald Trump's Letter to the President of Croatia

Sunday, July 15, 2018

Dear President of Croatia,

Just like prime minister Theresa May of Britain, you failed to take my advice on the best formulae your team were to use in their game against France. I told you that the fate of the White race was resting on your country's team. I told you that as a real estate developer in New York City, I knew a lot about those people from those shithole countries. I know how to scare the shit out of them. But you, a mere daughter of a butcher shop owner, ignored me. Look at the result now.

You did not just fail your country, you failed the great white race. Do you know how emboldened those godforsaken multiculturalists/globalists will be now? They will hold up the picture of France's team with the World Cup and try to sell it as the ideal. You are such a disgrace.

The good thing is that you and your country will go back to remain inconspicuous in world affairs. Who knows, your country may never get back to the World Cup final in fifty years. You squandered a rare opportunity because you didn't want to listen to Donald Trump. See your life now!

I blame myself for stooping so low to talk to you. You aren't even the most powerful person in your country. I should have been talking to your prime minister. You know what? I think in my speech at the UN this year, I should demand that all countries in the world should abandon the stupid parliamentary system and adopt the great American presidential system. When someone says he or she is president, we really know he or she is one. Not a president who travels at her own expense, flying economy class and watching World Cup soccer from the non-VIP stand. If any country opposes my idea, I will ban them from coming to New York City for the UN General Assembly.

Watch out! Before the next World Cup, my father's folks in Germany must get rid of that obnoxious woman at the helm of affairs in their country. And once again, Germany will come up with a pure white team that will thrill the world and restore the pride and the glory of our people.

Because you messed up, I am coming up with a brilliant idea. I am thinking of starting an alternative soccer competition to be called Trump's World Cup (TWC). Only the top twenty-five richest countries in the world will participate, eliminating insignificant countries like your Croatia, Uruguay, Costa Rica, and Iceland. Can you believe that the irrelevant Costa Rica knocked out the Great United States (GUS) from going to Russia for the finals?

Each participating country in the TWC will put up $40 million to be part of it. The winner takes home $1 billion, which is more meaningful than the pocket change FIFA gives now. I will put up the first $1 billion for the winner to take home. That, my friend, will preserve my name for eternity.

So there's no reason to waste more time writing you. Go back to the beach. Keep displaying your awful, disgusting bikini body that some dishonest people have been telling you is appealing. If you show a body like that anywhere near my Mar-a-Lago estate, I will ban you from coming to Florida.

Before I go, my people told me that you have been flirting with Iranian president Hassan Rouhani. You don't want to be in the line of fire and fury that Benjamin Netanyahu and I are planning to unleash on Iran. Some low-life people in your country may be calling you SWAMBO, as in, "she who must be obeyed." I don't need to advertise my capability, do I?

Yours truly,
Donald J. Trump
The 45th President of the United States of America

Donald Trump's 2nd letter to Vladimir Putin

Wednesday, July 18, 2018

Dear Vladimir Putin,

What a great summit we had, my friend. That was a historical one. Whatever happens from now on, we have made history. You and I are now the two greatest historical figures of the twenty-first century. Bar none. We have changed the course of world history for antiquity. The handshake in Helsinki has caused butterflies to blanket the skies of Europe and Asia. We are the new kids on the block determined to rewrite our histories in ways Lenin and George Washington could not have imagined.

We will change the world even more in the next seven years. That is my promise. And my words are my bond. By the time we are done, trust me, our statues will grace the great squares of the world, from Peru to Prague, from Casablanca to Karachi, from Tokyo to Tehran, from Sydney to Shanghai, from Phnon Penh to Pyongyang, and from Johannesburg to Jeddah.

As you can see, the busybodies here on American TV are displaying their moronic views once again. They want to know what we discussed in our private meeting. I trust that you will never let out the contents of the top-secret talks we had no matter the provocation. I hate leakers with the last fiber in me, so you can be sure that it won't leak from my side. I bet that you will take care of your interpreter the best Putinistic way you do those things. Mine has been taken care of the way the Trumps do things—which is in a sophisticated style.

Let me alert you that in days to come, we may have the need to use harsh words on Russia. These obsolete people around Washington, DC, may even force me to say some uncomplimentary stupid things about you. But you know they are just for the TV. You know that I hold you in the highest esteem. You are a great guy, and there is no other leader with your understanding of power, its use and essence, anywhere in the world—100 percent true. I have said to myself time and time again, if only they knew you, how wonderful you are, they would stop listening to the alarmists in Washington.

If need be, the Congress of the United States and the low IQ people who run some of the arms of my government may impose sanctions on Russia. You and I know they are meaningless gestures. Billions and billions of dollars will continue to flow between our two countries through the dark web located at the backyard of our great financial institutions. You are welcome to retaliate. You should make great noise about the danger of returning the Russia–US relationship to its antagonistic past to the detriment of our people. As usual, it will end there. Our communion in Helsinki is deep and eternal.

Melania sent her greetings. You know her parents' first choice of country to live in was Russia. Maybe when I come to Moscow later in the year, I will bring them with me.

Yours truly,
Donald J. Trump
The 45th President of the United States of America

Donald Trump's Letter to LeBron James

Saturday, August 4, 2018

Dear LeBron James,

My aides have pleaded with me to ignore you and your stupid antics. I have done so for a long time. My tongue rolls up spit, ready to volley it your way, but I restrain myself. Continuing to do so at this point would be an injustice to me. It will make me appear weak. And you know how I hate being seen as weak.

They said you are beloved in Ohio, a state I must win to be reelected. They also said that if our life stories were compared, there would be a contrast. I got the strategy outline they prepared. You were born dirt poor, while I was born super rich. You pulled yourself up by the bootstraps, while I got a one million-dollar head start. I heard them. They said you married your high school sweetheart, while I have dated and dumped more beauty queens than any other man in the world. All your three children were from one woman. On my part, I have married thrice, divorced twice, and had children with more than three different women.

Guess what! I don't give a damn! I need to take care of your ingratitude once and for all. You were born a loser. It was my fellow billionaire that gave you a chance to be somebody. Somehow, you seem to have horribly forgotten that. You should be eternally grateful to billionaires like me who make it possible for at-risk kids like you to be able to put food on your table. It is clear that if your life depends on your intellect, you will be spending time in a penitentiary somewhere in Ohio like your fellow inner-city travelers. At least, show some respect to us, your benefactors.

You built a little wacky school and childishly called it I Promise. And it got into your head. Ever heard of Trump University? Never mind. It is beyond your intellectual level. Do you know all the wonderful things my father and I have done for poor people from New York to Florida and from Florida to Virginia and from Virginia to Las Vegas? Tremendous acts of kindness. If you have any doubt, count the houses in New York alone that have Trump written on them. Do I brag about that? No. Do I get those TV vultures to come each time I cut a ribbon to open another house? No.

And about that talent thing… It is crazy how you people misuse the word *talent*. When we talk about people with talent, don't get it confused with people with muscles. Talent is what the founder of Facebook has. Muscles are what Mike Tyson has. Sorry, had. Talent is what Albert Einstein has. Muscles for laughter are what Chris Rock has. Those who can, do things. Those who can't, entertain those who do things.

Next time you feel you have something important to say, find a better TV channel. If you have no contacts at FOX News, let me know, and I will connect you to some fine and brilliant guys at FOX. Don't go near that fake news CNN. You can do better than that. And even if you must appear on CNN, stay away from stupid Don Lemon. Nothing will revamp Don Lemon's failing career. Not even if he gets an exclusive interview with Elvis, the King. Mr. Lemon is scum. He is not just obnoxious (if you know what the word means), but he is also so dumb, the morons at CNN just keep him there to fulfill affirmative action requirements. Something I hope Justice Brett Kavanaugh will get rid of as soon as he is confirmed to the US Supreme Court.

One last bit of advice. Forget what the dishonest media is telling you, listen to Laura Ingraham – shut up and dribble. You don't have another decade to do the only thing you were equipped to do. Oh, I forgot. You were also equipped to have babies, and I bet you are just getting started. Remember that they need to be fed. Don't count on food stamps. By the time I'm done with my second term, that benefit will be history. So if I were you, I would shut up and dribble.

I don't know the last time you read any book. Very likely not since you left high school. So, let me not trouble you with a long letter.

All the best,
Donald J. Trump
The 45th President of the United States of America

Donald Trump's Letter to Omarosa

Wednesday, August 22, 2018

Dear Omarosa,

Your book could not even crack the number one spot on Amazon's list of bestsellers despite the help I gave you? You lost so big. Shame on you!

Did you write it in Ebonics? Or were you so intoxicated by an evil desire to make me look bad that you lost the plot of your tale?

How could Rachel Hollis's *Girl, Wash Your Face* beat you on the bestseller list? Maybe she was saying to you, "Girl, wash your mouth and let some wise surgeon remove the cobwebs blanketing your tiny brain."

It is very sad that all my efforts to make you somebody were wasted attempts. Like all your people, you desired instant gratification instead of building on something that would last. You sold a couple of books, a few thousand at most, made enough money to visit your neighborhood salon and change your hairstyle. And then what?

Mark my words, this is exactly why you people can never be successful business people. In your own case, I have had reasons to question your mental stability. You were not really smart, but I had thought you had a bit of native intelligence that I could work with to turn you into something. But I guess when stupidity is

deeply buried in someone, no amount of exposure can neutralize it. Somehow, it finds a way to surface to the top.
    It was a huge mistake investing in you. Sad. Like John said, I just have to accept that some were not just born in the slum, but the slum was also born in them.

Yours truly,
Donald J. Trump
The 45th President of the United States of America

Donald Trump's Letter to Paul Manafort

Thursday, August 23, 2018

Dear Paul Manafort,

Y ou are a man's man, the pride of your Italian ancestors. You have given me hope to keep my faith in humanity. Despite the provocations by overzealous prosecutors, you took it like a man. At sixty-nine, you were a lot braver than that fifty-nine-year-old marine general Michael Flynn, who fell helplessly on his sword. What is eighty years in jail when you have, at most, another twenty years to live? They won't make you come back to the world to finish your sentence. Will they?

Beyond that, you know that I got your back. I do. With a stroke of the pen, I will make you a free man. And you bet that I will do it. When to do so and how is up to me. I'm still watching as things unfold. I'm letting them put up their best attack. When they are done, I will hit back. And you know how powerful my hit-backs are.

There is no need pardoning you for one conviction when other trials and convictions are coming. I feel that the best thing is for them to do their worst. Let them heap it all on you. One hundred years in prison, one thousand years in prison, it does not matter. Let the federal trial run its course. Let the state trial run its course.

And then, with a stroke of my pen, I will correct all the wrongs they have done on a good man like you and make you a free man again.

As a lawyer, you know that by wiping your slate clean, you can go on and enjoy the rest of your life as if nothing happened. Meanwhile, that traitor, Michael Cohen, will spend the rest of his life in squalor. I single-handedly took that motherfucker out of the Jewish squalor where I found him. And this is the thanks that I get?

We shall see how it ends. Believe me, it won't end like your father's. In your father's political profile as mayor of New Britain, it says, "Indicted but not convicted." I, Donald J. Trump, will leave your slate spotlessly clean. Nobody will mention in your biography that you even visited Ukraine, not to mention being tried and being convicted of a crime.

You worked for great historical individuals like Victor Yanukovych of Ukraine, Ferdinand Marcos of Philippines, Mobutu Sese Seko of Zaire and even guerrilla leader Jonas Savimbi of Angola. They are all great guys who live on in history books. You led my guerrilla campaign, slaying the so-called goliaths of the Republican Party. You are a nice man whose life is being ruined by that evil man Mueller.

Trust me, good will ultimately defeat evil. I defeated Crooked Hillary, and so will a good man like you ultimately defeat Evil Mueller.

As long as I am president, you don't have anything to worry about. For a loyal man like you who worked for presidents Ford, Reagan, and Bush Sr., you will be taken care of. And so, will your family. I am sure that you still have some money left from the $1 million a year Mobutu Sese Seko paid you in 1989 or the $950,000 a year that Ferdinand Marcos paid or the $1 million that the Nigerians paid you in 1991. Use it to keep your family going until I find an offshore account to send some money to your wife, Kathleen, and your two beautiful daughters.

Bill Clinton cheated like a dog, yet they did nothing to him – not even a slap on the wrist. I cannot allow them to destroy a business that you built with your sweat.

Rudolf t.g. Hess

Yours truly,
Donald J. Trump
The 45th President of the United States of America

Donald Trump's 2nd Letter to Michael Cohen

Thursday, August 24, 2018

Dear Michael Cohen,

Look at you. Loser. Look at how little you have become. I lifted you up, but you have no good brain to keep yourself there. You have no clue how massive my goodness was to you.

So, you recorded my conversations with you? I'm bigly disappointed. You are the worst form of scum on the earth! You are a lawyer from hell.

As Omarosa used to say, when I finish with you, you will know that hot water kills the tortoise.

Good riddance. And may you spend eternity in hell.

Yours truly,
Donald J. Trump
The 45th President of the United States of America

Donald Trump's Letter to Secretary of State Mike Pompoe

Friday, September 14, 2018

Dear Secretary of State Mike Pompoe,

This is just a draft.

I, Donald J. Trump, the 45th president of the United States of America, having done my best to make America great, and having resolved that America has failed to utilize my genius, do hereby resign the office of President of Make America Great Again.

Let America continue in its gradual decline until it is fully a subservient nation to the resurgent Russia and the rising state of China. And who knows, in another one hundred years, America may be taking orders from shithole countries like Nigeria. That would be a total disgrace.

I sort of hope that happens so that I will tell you all, "I told you so."

It is on record that I have warned America. My people are under the influence of criminals and rapists from Mexico and the Southern Hemisphere and from the voodoo of people from the shithole countries of Africa.

I have ordered an exorcist to come and remove the evil spirits left by that African that was last in the White House. I'm recommending a thorough disinfectant of the buildings before another American president goes in there. Otherwise, it would be the same outcome of putting in maximum effort for a meager result.

I will pray for the United States of America. The beautiful thing about my life is that I am very rich. Whatever happens, I will continue to live a fantastic life. I am going to have an unbelievable retirement. And when I die, I don't want any former president to come there and shed crocodile tears.

My enemies can smash my star on the Hollywood Walk of Fame. They can take anything away from me, my private jet, my Washington, DC, Hotel, my beloved Melania, but they can never take away the fact that I am, or should I say, was, the 45th president of the United States.

Yours truly,
Donald J. Trump
The 45th President of the United States of America

Donald Trump's Letter to His Son, Barron Trump

Sunday, September 16, 2018

My dear son, Barron,

I must apologize that I often forget that I have a 12-year-old son in the White House. For some strange reasons, not for a moment do I forget that I'm the president of these United States. I'm being 100% honest with you.

I know that Ivanka, Eric, Tiffney and Don Jr. will be alright. They are all grownups. Even when the whole world is going crazy, there is nothing that I do that they cannot make sense of. Don Jr., especially, has mastered my attitude and, even, my lingo.

Barron, you still have seven years to go before you will begin to understand the deeper meaning of everything that is happening around you today.

Despite what historians will write about me, just remember these undisputable facts. Your father is a great man. That is me, being modest. Naturally, I would have said that I'm the greatest president that ever lived, which is not far from the truth.

Contrary to what the liberal left is making of me, your father has unlimited human emotions. Yeah, I have emotions. I only show one on TV and when I tweet. I have fears, though you will never see it on my face – not even when the name Mueller is mentioned. Behind my public defiance, I'm just a kid like you who wants to belong and to be liked not just by the ignorant masses but also by those in high society.

I'm navigating with grace the headache of being president in the age of trolls. It is a peculiar challenge that Obama and Bush did not have to deal with. Despite my tough public exterior, you can attest to the fact that I am compassionate. I show kindness even to my most ardent opponent. Yes, I do. I don't obsess about them the way my tweets suggest.

I surrender to those who least expected me to. I conquer with ease those who are most steadfast against me. Beyond the insults, I'm just a teddy bear scrambling for a loving and lasting hug. I may not be the most humorous president but nobody will say that I don't try to keep America entertained.

My son, you know I am rich. But I'm not just rich in billions and billions of dollars; I also have a rich soul. I make sacrifices for the benefit of posterity. It will surprise those looking from outside that I am a reflective individual. Those who are introspectively impoverished make themselves feel good by thinking that I am superficial. I'm deep.

Barron, your father is deep. Your dad is smart. Don't forget that I graduated from Wharton Business School of University of Pennsylvania. It doesn't get better than that.

Beyond the ugliness of today's politics, history will record it on everlasting marble that I devoted my time as president to things that are more than myself. If people are patient enough, if they flip those things they think make me look small, they will see wisdom that they didn't know that I have.

My dear Barron, the world that you were born in is more complicated than the one I was born in. My job is to keep hope alive in America. When others are losing their heads, I stay strong and push ahead to that glorious future for you and our beloved country. Like a brave soul that I am, I do so without counting the loss to my reputation. It is only my temporary reputation that is hurt. My eternal reputation is sealed and secured far away from the reach of the wretched of this country.

One hundred years from now, my courage under this crushing pressure will be celebrated. Your dad would be identified as the hero who used bursts of energy, rage and genius, in that order, to quench what was once accepted as the inevitable decline of the American empire.

Keep this letter, my son. You may have reasons in the future to show it to the world to prove that you dad was a good man who did his very best for his country. That is all that our citizenship demands of us.

Despite all that I have said in this letter, being president of the United States of America is the best thing that can happen to any man. Eh, women, maybe not. If not for anything else, for the mere fact that as long as you are the president, behind your back, people can call you an idiot, a moron or complete narcissist but nobody can tell you to shut the fuck up.

My dear son, I have made my contributions to America. When you come of age, make yours. As for the verdict, if history gives me less than stellar report card, that history is bunker. It won't matter in the scale of things because the folks at Fox news will always get my back.

When they ask you what drove you dad, please tell them this. I'm driven by the fear of being nobody after all the efforts that I have put in the pursuit of happiness. It is for that reason that I am in constant pursuit of something, anything, that will secure a place for me here on earth, even when I'm gone. I'll not stop until I'm sure that 1000 years after the end of America, that I, Donald J. Trump, will remain somebody.

Yours truly,
Donald J. Trump
The 45th President of the United States of America

Acknowledgment

This is a unique book. It deals with an exceptional character, the president of the United States. It is not a first-hand account of what happened at the White House like James Comey's book or Omarosa's book. This book went deeper. Figuratively, it was a journey inside the head of president Donald Trump.

Unless one is a witch or a psychotherapist, which I am neither, the only other way to get into the head of another person is via brain surgery.

There are many people involved in performing brain surgery. Besides the lead surgeon, there are other neurosurgeons, neurologists, neuroradiologists, anesthesiologists, nurses, and other clinical professionals. Then, there are social workers, patient care coordinators, and others. Depending on the particular goal of the surgery, a dozen or more staff could be in the theater at once.

This particular surgery does not require the clipping off of an aneurysm. Neither did it require the removal of a tumor or abnormal brain tissue. Even entangled nerves and weak blood vessels were not tampered with. No electronic device was implanted. The surgeon simply took pictures of the various locations of the components and documented the findings.

I wish to thank Wiseguy for choosing me to convey this work to readers. I'm also grateful to a few people who read this work. You all contributed immensely in shaping what is finally presented here.

My wife, Edna, read the first piece that arrived, "A Letter to My Son's Teacher." She thought it deserved to be published. *The New Yorker*, *The Saturday Evening Post*, *The Atlantic*, *Slate*, *Huffington Post*, and so many other journals all begged to differ. Okay, I'm only guessing. I'm just looking for something to fill their silence.

But that silence did not stop other letters from coming through.

To my first reader, Mukami Kamau. You read them as they came – one after the other, week after week. Because you felt there was something in this before anybody else, I kept forwarding them as they came. Thank you for reading and for all your encouragement.

To the mogul John Nwabueze. I turned you into an editor – and a darned good one at that. Well done.

To Ekene Awuzie, your suggestions after a thorough read made this book a lot better.

To Okey Ndibe for being in the ring with me, night after night, cheering.

To all those cheering on the side, Rahman Oladigbolu, Chika Oduah, and Paul Onochie Modebe.

To my kids, Ije and Ogonna. This is the product of all those days of going to the library.

To my mother-in-law, Gold Veronica Onwunyi, for keeping it all together while I hustled.

To all those Fiverr freelancers who were too scared to record the voiceover of these letters in Donald Trump's voice. You all confirmed to me that there were some important things in this book.

To all the agents who did not even bother to respond to my query letters, I am truly thankful. You turned me into my own agent and publisher. Thank you for the confidence you had in me.

And most importantly, to all those who donated to my GoFundMe set up to support this publication- Declan Galvin, George Ezike, BU Nwosu, Francis Nwankwo, Johnson Obeke, Wumi Akintide, Andy F, Wayne Bassey, Perry Brimah, Theo Okanume, Alexie Njoku, Okey Ndibe, Olisa Adigwe, Fidelis Mkparu, Augustine Okoye, Raymond Ogamba, Francis Chukwu, Hyacienth Na'anmiap and the three people who do not want their names mentioned in a book like this.

Who is left?

About the Author

Rudolf t.g. Hess is the pen name of Dr. Damages, which is a pen name of Rudolf Ogoo Okonkwo, a New York City based journalist and satirist. He closely watched media coverage of Donald J. Trump before he was elected president. Since Trump became president, Mr. t.g. Hess has observed the shaking up of the norms of Washington, DC, America, and beyond. As someone who grew up under military dictators, he can see President Trump's soul from afar.

www.ingramcontent.com/pod-product-compliance
Lightning Source LLC
LaVergne TN
LVHW041337080426
835512LV00006B/497